THE BLOOD OF LÓÐURR AWAKENS

By Frank A. Rúnaldrar

HIGH GALDR SERIES
　　Book One: The Breath of Oðin Awakens (2nd Ed)
　　Book Two: The Spirit of Húnir Awakens (Part 1)
　　Book Three: The Spirit of Húnir Awakens (Part 2)
　　Book Four: The Blood of Lóðurr Awakens

QUESTIONS & ANSWERS SERIES
　　The Breath of Oðin Awakens - Questions & Answers
　　The Spirit of Húnir Awakens - Questions & Answers

THE BLOOD OF LÓÐURR AWAKENS

Norse Mysteries of Body, Soul & Shadow Self

by
Frank A. Rúnaldrar

Part of the High Galdr Series
www.highgaldr.com

Published in 2018 by:
Bastian & West
www.bastianandwest.com

Copyright © 2018 Frank A. Rúnaldrar

The moral right of the author has been asserted.

All rights reserved. No part of this publication may be reproduced or transmitted in any form or by any means, electronic or mechanical, including photocopying, recording, or by any information storage and retrieval system, without permission in writing from the copyright holder. Reviewers may quote brief passages.

Part of High Galdr Series
www.highgaldr.com

ISBN: 978-0-9955343-6-0

A CIP catalogue record for this book is available from the British Library.

Editor: James Millington
In-book illustrator: Ben Hansen
Original cover design: Judge a Cover Designs

Book typeset in Niva Light by PeGGO Fonts, Norse font by Joël Carrouché and runic elements in Felt-Tip Futhark by Thomas Kaeding

Copyright Notice: All rights, title and interests in the copyrights to all materials (including but not limited to any proprietary knowledge, data, information, manuals, illustrations, diagrams, flowcharts, marks or other information therein contained or thereby disclosed and representing the author's original works), are hereby reserved and to be considered the exclusive property of and belong exclusively to the author. The purchase of this book by any person(s), and its usage by any other party, shall not be construed as granting or conferring any rights by license or otherwise to the purchasing party or any other party who may come in possession of the book and/or its materials. No part of this publication or its materials may be reproduced, distributed, disseminated, or transmitted in any form or by any means and for any purpose, including but not limited to photocopying, recording, or other electronic or mechanical methods, without the prior written permission and consent of the author, except in the case of brief quotations embodied in critical reviews and certain other non-commercial used permitted by copyright law. In the event any reader or third party submits to the author or the publisher, either jointly or severally, any questions, then any questions based on, derived from or incorporating any of the author's materials in this publication, together with any answers provided by the author, if any, shall be deemed to be works derived from the author's copyrighted materials and accordingly such reader or third party in submitting its questions irrevocably agrees to the exclusive and royalty free world wide transfer and assignment (free of costs) of all or any rights, title or benefit in such questions to the owner for its discretionary use in any format and by any medium.

Usage Disclaimer: It is expressly agreed and acknowledged by all and any reader(s) and any parties that come into possession of the materials that all materials, information, techniques, methods, processes or statements made in this publication, and all and any associated materials as may be derived therefrom and distributed from time to time in any written or tangible forms and in any media (including electronic media), as the case may be, by the author or its publisher(s), are for to be used strictly for educational purposes only (the "Permitted Purpose") and not for any other personal or commercial purpose. All materials reflect the author's personal views and opinions, and no method or process or statement or anything else said in the materials is to be treated as having any scientific value, validity or status. Under no circumstances whatsoever or howsoever are any materials in this book, in whole or in part, intended to operate as scientifically proven methods, processes or statements, or intended to offer any medical or other advise, or be used in substitute for medical advise of and/or treatment by physicians for any matters. Neither the author nor its publisher(s) make any statement, representation, guarantee or undertaking howsoever or whatsoever as to the usefulness of any materials. The use of the materials for any other purpose, including any personal or commercial purposes other than for educational purposes, contrary to the Permitted Purpose, is not promoted and strictly prohibited. The author and its publisher(s) accept no risk, responsibility or liability for any unsanctioned use, which shall be at the user's sole risk, and shall, together and severally (the "Released and Indemnified Parties"), be held harmless and indemnified by any users engaging in any unsanctioned use contrary to this disclaimer from all and any claims, rights, liabilities, demands, obligations, conditions, promises, acts, costs, expenses, accountings, damages or actions of whatsoever kind or nature, whether in law or otherwise, whether known or unknown, which they made have or may thereafter have against the Released and Indemnified Parties for or by any reason of any occurrence, matter or thing which arise or are claimed to have arisen out of or in connection with any such unsanctioned use of the materials.

I would like to dedicate this to all those who walk besides me here in Midgard...

Table of Content

The Blood of Lóðurr Awakens
- Definitions of Norse Terms I
- The Norse Tradition - Heritage of The Indo-Europeans .. VII
  - The Eddas VII
  - The Saga(s) X

The Energetic Level of the Self
- The Energetic Trinity of the Self 1
  - The Body (Lik), Energy Body (Hamr) and Shadow (Sal) 4
- The Gifts of Lodurr (in the Eddas) 9
- Norse View of the Creation of Man 13
  - Insights Into the Nature of Midgard (Earth) 21
- Our Bodies – Our Foundational Seed 25

Biological Awareness
- The Physical Body (Lik)
  - Foundation for Biological Awareness 37
  - Body Awareness – Biological Awareness 43
  - Functions of Biological Awareness 47
  - Awakening the Bodily Awareness & Intelligence . 51
  - Expanding Biological Awareness 59
    - Óðr Merging into Biological Awareness 63
    - Runic Flow into the Biological Awareness 63
  - Activating Spiritual Biological Awareness 67
    - Stage II: Forming the Óðrerir Outer Boundaries 68

Biological Awareness – Back to Basics
- Overview of Enhancement 77
  - Body Types 77
  - Learning to Shadow via Physical Body 79
  - Body Shapes as Energy Indicators 81

IMPACT OF BODY FORM – THE THREE FUNDAMENTAL FORCES......85
   A FEW WORDS ON MUSCLE 90
   A FEW WORDS ON THE NERVOUS SYSTEM 92
SANCTITY OF THE BODY 95
BODY AND MEDIATION 97

MYSTERIES OF BLOOD AND DNA

BLOOD – CRYSTALLISED MEGIN AND LIFE ESSENCE 103
   BLOOD AND THE PHYSICAL BODY (LIK) 104
   ENERGETIC NATURE OF BLOOD 106
   BLOOD AND 'PERSONALISED' LIFE FORCE 107
BLOOD IN THE TRADITIONAL CONTEXT 111
BLOOD AND THE RUNES 113
   EMBODIMENT OF RUNIC ENERGY INTO THE BLOOD 114
HUMAN DEOXYRIBONUCLEIC ACID (DNA) 121
   PURPOSE OF DNA 123
   VIBRATING THE DNA WITH MEGIN 129
SÓL (SOWILO) DNA ACTIVATION 131

INTENT

MASTERING INTENT – PART II 139
MASTERING INTENT – PART III 143
   PULLING THE SELF INTO THE LIK 145

THE ENERGY BODY (HAMR)

ENERGY BODY (HAMR) FUNDAMENTALS 151
   THE CYCLE OF EXISTENCE OF THE HAMR 153
   BIRTH OF THE HAMR 154
   DEATH OF THE HAMR 157
THE HAMR IN EDDIC AND TRADITIONAL SOURCES 165
ENERGY BODY COHESION AND SHAPING 169
   PREPARING THE ENERGY BODY FOR USE 172
   THE SILVER CORD 173
   SHAPE OF THE HAMR 174
   INTENDING THE HAMR 175
   EMPOWERED WITH INTENT 177
PERCEIVING THE ENERGY BODY (HAMR) 179
BIOLOGICALLY AWARE HAMR 185
SENSING THE ENERGY OF THE ENERGY BODY SPHERE 191

CONNECTING WITH THE ENERGY BODY (HAMR) 193
    ESTABLISHING THE CONNECTION 195
    GENDER ADVANTAGES 196

THE SHADOW SELF (SAL)
INTRODUCING THE SHADOW SELF (SAL) 201
    WHAT THE SAL IS NOT 202
    UNDERSTANDING THE SAL 204
    FUNCTIONS OF THE SAL 205
    SAL – THE DARK SIDE OF OUR SELF 207
CONNECTING WITH THE SAL 209
USING THE SAL AND GAINING CONTROL 213
    NOTES ON ADVANCED SHADOW (SAL) WORK 217
TRIANGULAR RELATIONSHIP: PHYSICAL (LIK)
SHADOW (SAL) – ENERGY (HAMR) 219

APPENDIXES
APPENDIX A: TABLE OF RUNIC NAMES IN
    ICELANDIC & GERMANIC 229

APPENDIX B: REFERENCES & FOOTNOTES 233

APPENDIX C: DANGERS OF WIFI
    TO HUMAN HEALTH AND DNA 241

FORTHCOMING TITLES 247

Table of Illustrations

Self at the energetic level 2
Female body shapes 83
Male body shapes..83
Flow Force body shapes 88
Solidifying Force body shapes................88
Burning Force body shapes 89
DNA Strand..122
Silver Cord structure when projecting 174
Trance & Meditation (sitting) position 179
Spherically shaped energy body...........................180
Egg shaped energy body..180
Spherically shaped energy body............................191
The shadow (Sal) located at the bottom left........202
The Shadow body (Sal)
    emanating from within 204
Fully Formed Shadow Self (Sal)..............................215

Notes from the Author

It is with great pleasure that I present you with the final book leading into High Galdr itself. In this title, we are going to look at the physical body (Lik), the energy body (Hamr) and the shadow (Sal). These are the final and yet most important parts of our Self, and they are the foundation from which we all rise, for the human being is a physical Being first and foremost and a spiritual Being second. Do not see this as a bad thing – it is a blessing whose meaning will only become clear to those who work through their physicality. This part of the Self is also the foundation into which we ground our runic practices in order to manifest tangible results in our Self and in our environments.

I have tried to carefully cover all the basics leading into the more advanced work within these pages. It was a challenge I hope I have lived up to, because for me the advanced practices are the basics. This has forced me to work backwards but if it helps you to get to mastery, every ounce of effort was most definitely worth it, in my eyes. You should find within a complete guide to work through. By the time you are done with these practices, you will have advanced far beyond just the goal of preparing for High Galdr.

Do not despair when things get hard and take time. They are supposed to – never give up and keep at it! Here is where you, as a seed in creation, start to germinate into your future Self. The two are brought together into ONE. This is the secret to the unity, as it is always found within, not in others. Midgard is a garden, and mankind are the seeds – what will each of you become? Fascinating to see!

Most importantly, enjoy the journey! Have fun with it. It is the adventure of a lifetime and you are taking your first steps within the Big Picture. May your bodies be strong, your energy bodies shine brightly and your shadows dance around you, all as ONE, and beautify creation in its own right!

Definitions of Norse Terms

All terms used refer to their original Old Norse or Proto-Germanic meanings not their modern day derivatives in the Scandinavian, German or Icelandic languages.

Önd – Part of the psycho-spiritual construct of the Self as viewed in Norse mysticism and mythology, the Önd sits at the apex of the spiritual level of the Self and can be loosely described as 'The Breath of Oðin' or luck / Megin-fulled breath.

Óðr (or Óðr, or Óð) – Part of the psycho-spiritual Self-sitting at the apex of the mental part of the Self, it can be loosely thought of as the conscious awareness or totality of the spirit.

Hugr – The Hugr is often thought of as the reasoning or logic part of the mind, sometimes as the mind itself and often as the intellect or intellectual capacity of the mind. Essentially it is the manifestation of the active characteristics of the (Spirit) Óðr.

Minni – The polar opposite of the Hugr and often thought of as the root of memory, the Minni is actually the individual record of one's experiences and acts as an anchor point for those events.

Hamr – The Hamr is the energy body, often described as the blueprint of the physical.

Lik – Part of the psycho-spiritual Self sitting at the apex of the energetic part of the Self, the Lik is the complete physical body as a result of the fusion of matter and spirit via the medium of energy. When talking about the Lik we include everything which is part of it, including the energetic and spiritual elements as well as the typically physical ones such as blood, DNA, nervous system and so forth.

Sal – Part of the psycho-spiritual self sitting at the bottom of the energetic part of the Self, the Sal is often loosely translated as the 'shadow'. In effect, it is the complimentary opposite of the Hamr.

Heimdall – One of the principle Gods in Norse mythology, Heimdall was described as the white god or whitest of the gods. He is linked to light and the pure power thereof. He possesses the resounding horn Gjallarhorn, which he will sound at the time of Ragnarök. He is the God responsible for originating the various classes of mankind and imbuing these with increasing degrees of divinity.

The Æsir – This refers to the clan of Gods from Ásgarð, typically associated with the divine aspects of spiritual origin. They are wielders of the Galdr sciences (use of runes and their correct applications) and have strong connections with the spiritual, awareness, intellect, mind, knowledge and the sciences.

The Vanir – The Vanir refers to the clan of Gods from Vanaheim, typically associated with the natural order of things and having strong connections with nature, the world and the physical as it moves towards the spiritual. They are wielders of Seidr crafts (sorcery, divination, soothsaying, shamanistic practices, herbal medicines and so forth).

Yggdrasil (Mjötvið) – The mythical Ash tree that is home to the nine worlds in Norse cosmology. It is also thought of as being the foundation of the cosmos itself and everything within it.

Egil's Saga – Otherwise termed in Iceland as the Egla, this is an Icelandic Saga dating back to 1240 AD, which details the life of Egil Skallagrimsson a farmer, Viking and poet.

Muspelheim – Muspelheim was the first world to be formed out of the great emptiness called Ginnungagap. It is a realm of flame, fires, light and explosive power unreachable by any not native to it.

Húnir (Hœnir) – One of the Æsir Gods, he helped create mankind along with Oðin and Lóðurr. He gave the first man and woman Óðr and hence imbued them with spirit. He is also one of the Gods who survives Ragnarök and gains prophetic powers thereafter.

Njörðr – Vanir god of the Sea, he is the father of Freya and Frey and was one of the hostages exchanged in the Æsir-Vanir war. It is said he will return to head the Vanir after Ragnarök.

Lóðurr (Lóð or Lóðr) – Lóðurr is a mysterious God, whom academics seem unable to accept other than trying (and failing) to identify him with Loki or even Freyr. He gives the first man and woman blood and hence health, in other words flesh or physicality.

Ragnarök – Also known as the Twilight of the Gods, this final battle was foretold in the Völuspá (stanza 41). It describes the ultimate fate of the Gods themselves.

Ætts – Meaning 'clan', it can also refer to related grouping of concepts, individuals or sets of people. It is sometimes referred to as kin-Ætts which would be used in terms of a grouping of related people. For instance, Ætts in terms of individuals would include related individually such as family, whereas kin-Ætts would expand this to a wider set of relations such as an entire clan.

Norns – This typically refers to the Jotun (giantess) sisters Urð, Verðandi and Skuld who weave the threads of fate for men and gods alike. They also draw water from the Well of Urð and collect sands from around it to pour on the Yggdrasil to prevent it from rotting. The word Norn can also refer to the concept of the fate weaver attached to individuals at birth which could be either good or bad, weaving either a fortunate or unfortunate fate for that individual.

Niflheim – One of the Nine Worlds in Norse Cosmology, Niflheim is a world of primordial ice and cold, sometimes also called the mist world.

Fylgja – Part of the archetypal level of the Self, the Fylgja is a spirit which binds to the individual, becoming a part of him or her upon birth. It is always inherited down the ancestral lines and carries experiential essence and memories and powers of the former Self's embodiment. The Fylgja forms into either animal, humanoid or geometric form depending on evolutionary progress of both the individual and itself.

Kin-Fylgja – Similar to the Fylgja, this overarching spirit carries the experiential essences of the entire family line, the sum resulting from the entire ancestral lines up to the current point. It attaches to the eldest male of the family line and communicates primarily through the females of the line.

Hamingja – The Hamingja is part of the archetypal level of the Self. It manifests as an energetic organ in the individual which stores the Megin (power) it produces from various runic and life energies.

Wyrd and Ørlǫg – This refers to fate or rather threads of fate as they flow through creation. Cosmically, Ørlǫg is seen as infinite fibres of energetic substance flowing throughout all existence. From a human perspective, these fibres appear to flow through Creation but also through individuals, Gods and all life forms, setting the path they will follow over the course of their existence. However, when viewed from a Cosmic perspective, all things in Creation flow through the fibres. The Wyrd refers to these threads on a larger scale such as for humanity as a whole, individual races and clans while Ørlǫg refers to how these threads manifest on the individual level. The Wyrd is formed by the Norns and the Ørlǫg is build from the Wyrd based on individual's power, fate and evolutionary needs by the Fylgja.

Óðrerir (Odhrærir, Óðrørir) – This refers to the container or cauldron which holds the sacred mead. Its equivalent is the legend of the 'Holy Grail' in Arthurian mythology and the 'Holy Chalice' in Christian mythology. The Óðrerir may well have been the inspiration for these later myths.

The Norse Tradition - Heritage of The Indo-Europeans

It is impossibly difficult to determine the full extent of or to search out all sources of the Norse tradition. Most pre-date the widespread availability of writing, while others were passed exclusively from one generation to the next orally. The main sources of knowledge left to us in this modern day and age are found in the Eddas and the Sagas.

The Eddas

The term 'Eddas' comes from Old Norse and it is used by modern-day students and academics to refer to two main Icelandic literary works that serve as the basis of our knowledge of Norse mythology, tradition, teachings and history.

There are two primary Eddas, both written during the 13th Century in Iceland. The first set is grouped under the label 'Poetic Eddas', which predate even the Viking Age, and come from an unknown source.

They are divided into two sections; the first is a narration of the creation, destruction and rebirth of the world and provides the mythology of the Norse deities as well. The second is a set of legends relating to Norse heroes, kings and wise men.

The Poetic Eddas were incorporated into the Codex Regius written during the 13th century. Unfortunately, it was not until the mid-1600s that the Codex resurfaced in the hands of Brynjólfur Sveinsson, a bishop to the Church of Iceland in Skálholt. Brynjólfur was also a scholar at heart, hence his fascination with the old myths and legends! It is he who collected and produced this compilation of Old Norse mythology and heroic poems into the Eddas. However, it is widely accepted that he was not their author and so they were not labelled after him. He gifted his findings to King Christian IV of Denmark in manu-script form, thus earning it the name Codex Regus, which was then preserved in the Royal Library until 1971 when a formal return was made to Iceland.

The second Eddas were compiled from traditional oral sources and (theorised to be derived from) an unknown set of Eddas often referred to as the Elder Eddas by Icelandic scholar Snorri Sturluson (dated from the 14th century). He collated these literary works under the label of Prose Eddas. Like the Poetic Eddas, the Prose Eddas also describe in detail the creation, destruction and rebirth of the world, Norse mythology and life. Due to his background and the time period in which Snorri lived, the 'Christianisation' of certain concepts and legends are to be found in this text. Nonetheless, it does provide an invaluable and rich account of the Norse tradition and, just as importantly, how it was recounted over the generations.

Scholars have long held the view that the Poetic Eddas, and therefore the Prose Eddas, came from a much older source. The rediscovery of what is known as the Elder Eddas helped confirm that suspicion. The Elder Eddas are comprised of the Pagan poems and teachings that were later hinted at in Snorri's Prose Eddas.

Many translations from Old Norse can be found and the number thereof seems to increase steadily over time. One key point to keep in mind is that the Eddas are complex literary works detailing the Norse tradition through poetry and prose. Accordingly, when reading various translations, different terms and words are often found to express the same underlying concept or similar words are used to describe totally different ones. Add to this the fact that many Old Norse terms have no equivalents in modern day languages, and it becomes vitally important to read in between the lines, so to speak, referring back to the concept rather than relying strictly on the words themselves. A literal, legalistic reading that has become completely engrained in the modern readers' minds will fail to capture the actual meanings, concepts and knowledge held within the Eddas.

Aside from those mentioned, other so-called Eddas can be found. These are typically adaptations in use by specific groups based on either the Prose or Poetic Eddas. The key point to note, however, is that those are adaptations.

The translations of the Prose and Poetic Eddas that have been used as source materials for this work can be found in both the references and further reading sections. Modern day adaptations and/or derivatives are not used.

The Saga(s)

Unlike the Eddas, the term Saga (story) refers to one of the many stories, poems, legends and so forth. Not all the Sagas made it into the Eddas. Individual Sagas might have not been discovered until a much later, post-Eddas compilation period.

These Sagas are individual tales in prose or poetic form detailing historical events of heroic deeds, tales or important persons (a great many of them Vikings, Pagans or even sometimes Christians), bishops, saints and even legendary heroes. Many of the Sagas include tales of kings, special individuals (such as the Egil Sagas used in this text), and even territorial historic events ranging from the Nordic countries to the British Isles, France and even North America (Canada in particular)[1]. Their main characteristic is that they are a historical statement or tale (that is the literal meaning of the term Saga). This has raised much speculation as the intellectual machinery attempts to digest material that is these days considered to be supernatural or metaphysical.

This range of subject matter is simply due to the fact that these records were, more often than not, kept within individual families, transmitted orally or simply brought from a different territory. Remember, the Old Norse people (Indo-Europeans) existed long before the Viking age and had to survive forced Christianisation, dispersion of territories, hostile natural environments, and so forth. In other words, these Sagas provided additional insights into the traditions, mythology, legends and teachings that were initially transmitted orally and then, once writing became widely available, were from time to time published. Even to this date, however, many of the Sagas have never been published and are kept from public view for a variety of reasons. Some of these reasons are of a very practical nature. In Iceland, for instance, these stories are considered to be part of the national heritage, hence books or manuscripts that are valued as family heirlooms, if known about, would be confiscated by the state on the basis of it being a national treasure. This is somewhat of an over-simplification but is an example of one of the many reasons why a lot of these Sagas never have (and most probably never will) see the light of public accessibility or dissemination. Others might hold deep-seated hereditary knowledge, which, more often than not, requires specific genetic and energetically transmitted capabilities to be of any use. This is the case with the higher mysteries bestowed upon the Jarls by Heimdall.

Fortunately, many Sagas are available for public consumption, and they do provide an exceptional insight into the wisdom and traditions of our ancestors. In this work, the Sagas are used to illustrate and gain further insights into teachings from older sources, be they part of the oral tradition or those in the Eddas[2].

This seeming endless diversity of sources is what makes studying the Old Norse tradition wildly exciting and fascinating beyond expectation, yet also insanely frustrating. Each Saga and Edda can expand our understanding, yet finding the relevant ones can be a most noteworthy challenge, in addition to actually understanding the knowledge therein once it is found! Nevertheless, gaining a solid foundation into the tradition is key; it is after all part of our heritage and is what empowers us. The appendices will provide more references and recommended reading. Fear not, however — all Eddas and Sagas relevant to the topics and teachings in this book have been included; for without basing such teachings in the actual texts and other sources of heritage they would hold no validity per se. It is of vital importance to work with these Eddas and Sagas as the foundation upon which we build our spiritual heritage.

THE ENERGETIC LEVEL OF THE SELF

The Energetic Trinity
Of The Self

We now enter into the domain of Lóðurr and the Self upon the energetic level. At this stage, the Self has manifested from its initial Spark in the archetypal (see *The Breath of Oðin Awakens*), through the mental level (see *The Spirit of Húnir Awakens*) to finally ground itself in manifested reality: the energetic level, which is what *The Blood of Lóðurr Awakens* covers.

One thing which seems very difficult for people to understand, which we should clarify immediately from the word go, is that the physical is PART of the energetic level of reality (and Self). Many mistakes over the course of time have been made where the physical was somehow seen as something separate and an end point of manifestation. In those misconceptions, people are led to believe that the energetic manifests eventually as the physical, where the latter is somehow on a lower level than the former. Time to brush away those misconceptions. In the Norse tradition, the physical is BOTH part and parcel of the energetic level of reality AND its very centre (hence Midgard being the central point in

Creation). We know this as well from science – more and more evidence is starting to point to the underlying energetic structures and mechanisms of our physical world. We will be looking at Einstein's e=mc2 and its implications to the energetic-matter dynamics in terms of the runes and their mysteries. For now, let us first and foremost look at the Norse teachings.

Self at the energetic level

We see the holy trinity manifest yet again within this part of the Self as the physical body (Lik), the energy body (Hamr) and the shadow Self (Sal). Looking at this distribution, some might wonder why the physical body (Lik) is at the upper root. The answer is extremely simple: everything starts and ends with the physical body (Lik). Shock horror! Right? This is why most people do not perceive the energetic levels of reality: you have the Spirit (Óðr) -> physical body (Lik) connection from peak of mental to peak of energetic, but the consciousness itself is born within the physical. You can perceive and be aware with only Spirit (Óðr) but not fully consciously as we understand it. **The quality of conscious awareness is born within the physical part of reality.** In order to reach a more direct interaction with said energetic levels, we need to gradually extend our consciousness AND awareness down the triangular relationships to include the energetic body (Hamr), or blueprint, to be exact. We can also follow the other side of growth and go downwards, expanding within the shadow Self (Sal). Please note, the Sal refers to both the shadow Self and/or the shadow body. Since the latter is mainly a Seiðr practice, we will only deal with the minimum necessary for runic work and leave the in-depth look at the shadow Self and its reality for Seiðr teachings. Ultimately, you will need to master both in order to integrate the energetic trinity of the Self.

So why is everyone not automatically aware of the energetic via their energy body (Hamr)? It is simply a matter of limited awareness, mental focus and habituation not to. You will need to reach the energy body (Hamr) and stir it into activity. Its default function is to act as a blueprint for the cellular regeneration in your physical body (Lik). We will, over the following sections, look at each of these parts of the Self and how to gain control of them – as well as how to kick them into action! Our starting point is the physical body (Lik), where you will learn what mysteries it holds, why it is SO important and how it is the foundation of shape and Being in the entire Self across ALL its manifestations.

The Body (Lik), Energy Body (Hamr) and Shadow (Sal)

There seems to be an ongoing confusion of concepts when it comes to the energy body (Hamr) and the physical body's (Lik) energy systems. Most people (actually, the vast majority) confuse the two. This is why a lot of practices fail to manifest any tangible results, they are targeted at the wrong place. The physical body (Lik) can best be thought of as an electro-chemical organism composed of micro-organisms (cells, viruses, bacteria and so forth). It is true that the energy flow through the body has underlying patterns and respective pathways – no sensible person can argue with that, as every nerve in the body uses and generates electrical impulses which in turn also produces electro-magnetic fields. Our bodies are electric devices (which is why they are sensitive to all sorts of electro-magnetic fields and their interferences) with a biological basis. This naturally gives us a whole energetic side to our bodies which can be manipulated by all sorts of energies harnessed physically (think about medical scanners). Additionally, it is important to keep in mind that energy is energy, so therefore we can use energetic practices to influence the energetic components of our bodies. However, all this does not mean that using methods to affect our energy body (Hamr) is equivalent to those targeting the energy components/systems of the physical. These two do indeed share – let us call them – connecting points or junctions of sorts, but they are not one and the same.

This is one of the main reasons when people try to influence the actual energy body (Hamr) it produces no tangible results, their runic energy ends up being targeted at the energy systems of the physical body (Lik) and is simply absorbed by it. The counter problem is also present when people try to influence the physical body (Lik) with energy, it too fails to produce results (most often). Why? Because the way they are using those energies is how you would do so when targeting the energy body (Hamr), not the physical. All you get in those cases is that the energy will neither end up in the one nor the other, and will be grounded or eventually dissipate.

Getting to grips with the separation of the physical and energy bodies is key, otherwise not only will you fail to affect the one you are aiming for but you will end up in the usual confusing mess when it comes to dealing with things such as the Hvels (energy vortexes similar to the Eastern concept of chakras) and with the physical body (Lik)'s energy storage centres. This is also why there are so many different accounts of how many of these there are, where they are located, and so forth. The modern-day literature on these topics is a total mess and those in the know remain silently watching whilst being amused. The Hvel will not be discussed in any significant depth here due to lack of space. They will hopefully be the subject of a publication of their own.

To make matters worse, the energy body (Hamr) does overlap the physical – actually, the latter is INSIDE the energy body, its central point. The best way to conceptualise it is to remember that the energy body's outer boundary (or skin, if you prefer) is your auric field (or bubble). In most people, it has the shape of a sphere; the entire thing is the energy body (Hamr). We have up to this point dealt with it as being inside the physical. This is where the core of it is but the entire energy body (Hamr) includes everything up to the outer shell of what we refer to these days as the auric field. When you are working with the part inside the physical, as you did in *The Spirit of Húnir Awakens – Part 1*, you are working with its core – think of it as its heart or brain if that helps. The rest of it constantly radiates outwards into a spherical shape. Because of our socially indoctrinated obsession with physicality, our energy body (Hamr) condenses in the same space as the physical body (Lik). Over generations, this phenomenon has resulted in changes to the energy body (Hamr) where its point of centrality has shifted into a type of fluid shape within the physical, where it subsequently concentrated part of its energy, hence producing the 'core' you feel as that layer immediately under your skin. When you did the practice 'Óðr (Spirit) Projection'[3] and sat still for a while, you would feel the energy pulsating outwards all over your physical body (Lik)'s skin, radiating outwards. That radiation extends itself throughout the entire sphere of your energy body (Hamr) and is typically interpreted as an 'auric' field emanating outwards. This, as you can imagine, leaves all too many practices 'up in the air' because they ignore a rather large portion of the energy body (Hamr).

You might wonder where that leaves the shadow body (Sal). That is an altogether different matter. The shadow body (Sal) is found in the 'gaps' in-between the energy and physical bodies. Hence it is bound to the physical shape. The energy body (Hamr) is what most traditions refer to as the 'soul'. **It is a product of the inherited genetics and the imprints of the Spirit (Óðr) and Fylgja.** This is why there are so many key differences between those of different racial backgrounds. The most well known is Easterners having seven chakras whereas Westerners (those of Indo-European heritage) have nine Hvels, and so forth.

This very structure and separation of the physical and energy body is what allows those unfortunate ones to be soulless and still remain alive. It is also what makes it necessary for each of us to reach the energy body (Hamr) and why it is not readily accessible to our conscious minds or influences. It is also what takes over at the point of death of the physical, and it too eventually fades out of existence, because without the physical body (Lik) to provide it energy, there is nothing else to nourish it. Traditionally, in old literature, this used to be termed the 'second death'. In the section dealing with the energy body (Hamr), we will see how to awaken it and at a later point in time how to make it self-sufficient in order to allow us to use it consciously and bypass this second death.

# The Gifts of Lóðurr (in The Eddas)

We enter into the domain of the final of the three Gods' gifts, having looked at Oðin's in *The Breath of Oðin Awakens* and Húnir's in *The Spirit of Húnir Awakens - Parts 1 & 2*. It is time to delve into the gifts of Lóðurr.

Unlike the former Gods, Lóðurr does not give one but two gifts to Ask and Embla (the first man and woman). Depending on the translation used, different meanings are given and most of these are debated amongst academics. For our purposes, we will look at their original meanings and their energetic impacts. This will provide us with a far more accurate definition than any non-energy-aware academic will ever reach, as we base them in energetic reality rather than in purely intellectual terms and human perceptions (which are far from flawless).

In the Völuspá, stanza 17 the Völva recounts how the original human beings were taken from being trees to human. Interestingly, those who suffer from what is termed *epidermodysplasia verruciformis*, a rare immune system disorder, seem to revert to the having tree-like characteristics. This condition, which increases susceptibility to the HPV virus, can trigger bark-like skin warts to grow all over the body, eventually preventing use of limbs and movement (commonly called the 'tree man syndrome'). Ask and Embla were given lá and litu góða by Lóðurr (as mentioned in stanza 18). The literal interpretation, or as close as we get to it, would be 'softness' for lá and 'good colouring' for litu góða.[4] The translator here points out that lá is 'the line of foam that edges the shore' and that in one of the Sagas, it refers to complexion. In view of the fact that both Ask and Embla were trees (Ash and Elm trees respectively), it would make sense for it to be associated with softness. Otherwise, the tree forms would not be able to move! This motion which we have is essential. It goes a little further than simple motion. A vast range of forms of awareness (Beings) in creation are static — they do not move, but instead, they project parts of their own static forms out. Picture it as a vast space filled with static immobile forms dispersed throughout endless uniform space. By giving softness and the underlying ability of softer shapes to take on distinct forms and to reshape, we get to the point where motion becomes possible. This key characteristic of mobile awareness is what we see as a key building block in the formation of our energy body (Hamr)'s awakening. When we learn to MOVE our own energy bodies (Hamr), we fully awaken. An interesting parallel can be drawn from the name of the God himself: Lóðurr. Its exact meaning is unknown but it can be linked to Gothic words referring to growth, shape and the German lodern meaning 'to blaze'. All these words relate to shaping and expansion (via the blaze reference which grows and expands) and since all the Gifts of these Three Gods indicate the giving of their Self to Ask and Embla, it makes sense that this would also be the case with Lóðurr's gifts.

The other gift: litu góða is translated by Dronke[5] as 'comely hues' and by Thrope[6] as 'goodly colour' but can also refer to good shape. The colour or hue interpretation is the most accurate when looking at things energetically. The underlying reason for this is that initially, all humans had a dark brown energy colour (a very earthly-grounded energy type). This eventually shifted into the overwhelming white energy we have today. Some individuals still have loamy brown or Champagne-coloured energy but for the vast majority, it is either at or moving towards a white. From the white, which is nothing more than a transitory energy, it will change into a completely different one, depending on what next step of evolution is taken. This is why colour is the most correct interpretation – it related to Lóðurr's gift which has taken the darkest brown energy towards the white in order to allow it to transition to something else. Human energy is being 'purged' with 'the blazing' gifts so that it can transition from one type to another. Think of it as the 'ultimate' alchemy!

Before leaving the translation discussion, it is important to look at Thrope's translation of the term lá when he equates it with blood rather than shape. It might seem odd but there is foundation in his thinking. Blood, as we will see, is the crystallisation of personalised life force and Megin (power), a biological manifestation of both energy (the personalised life force) and an energy-life carrier (the power element). Blood and form (or shape) connect at the junction which dictates that "The flow of energy through a system tends to organise that system"[7]. Because blood is the life energy carrier, how it flows through the system (in this case, the physical body (Lik)) determine its shape and its underlying functions. It is a far more obscure translation but one worth keeping in mind due to its hints at underlying energetic reality. Ultimately, it matters not whether you view Lóðurr's gift as one of blood or shape because they are both so interrelated that the one gives rise to the other. It is worth noting that the blood of a tree can be thought of as being its sap – hence in their tree forms, they would have had some form of blood already but with a hard, ridged shape or skin. Food for thought...

One important distinction between the Gifts of all three Gods is that in Lóðurr's case, he makes two gifts rather than one, as did Oðin and Húnir. This is in direct compliance with the principles of manifestation, which dictate that the energetic level of reality is where duality comes into play and is needed for full manifestation to take place. Since he is affecting the physical (densest level of the energetic), he has to conform to the rules of the energy level of reality and hence make two gifts. Each of them impacts and counteracts the other. Shape determines movement and flow of expression, and the intensity of that shape's movement determine vibration, which in turn influences the colour of its energy – simple and highly effective. Through their interaction, the 'third' is born, which is greater than the original two. For those who can make sense of this interaction in this context, a great key is to be found within these words.

This all reflects perfectly in the study of this level of the Self, where we have the Lik, Hamr and Sal in play. It is now time to delve into each of those.

Norse View of The Creation of Man

The Human being is a rather odd being, according to the Norse mythologies. We have several highly complex ancestries to contend with on a spiritual, energetic and physiological level.

The *Gylfaginning* and *Skáldskaparmál* outline how the first world to come into existence was Muspelheim (Múspellsheimr or Múspell) in the south and is a fiery uninhabitable region by non-natives. After 'many ages', Niflheim was formed.[8]

Third (Oðin in one of his many disguises) states that "just as from Niflheim there was coldness and all things grim, so what was facing close to Muspelheim was hot and bright, but Ginnungagap was as mild as a windless sky".

When the hot air met the rime, it melted and dripped, and as it did, it fell into the shape of a man who was Aurgelmir (otherwise known as Ymir). From him the Jötnar (giants) descended. When asked if Ymir was a god, the High replies that by no means would he be considered one and that "he was evil and all his descendants".

We then learn from the *Poetic Eddas* in *Grímnismál*, where Oðin (disguised as Grímnir) reveals that "Of his bones the hills, of his hair the trees" were made.[9] The key part to keep in focus is the fact that we are told from what his hair trees (in other translations: trees and plants) were made. This means that Yggdrasil, being the mother tree, was also made from his hair AND so were human beings – remember, Ask (which means Ash) and Embla ('elm') were trees originally.

In stanza 17 of the *Völuspá*, the Völva states that Oðin, Hœnir and Lóðurr found Ask and Embla on land. The Völva says that the two were capable of very little, lacking in Ørlög, and tells us that they were given gifts by the three Gods.[10]

We later find out that humans were also originated from Heimðall when he fathered the three classes of mankind.

Interestingly, in *Gylfaginning*, the High explains that dwarfs were created from Ymir's flesh as maggots which grew in his flesh. The Gods then, when holding their Thing[11], "discussed where the dwarfs had been generated from in the soil and down in the earth like maggots in flesh. The dwarfs had taken shape first and acquired life in the flesh of Ymir and were then maggots, but by decision of the gods, they became conscious with intelligence and had the shape of men though they live in the earth and in rocks". Stanzas from Völuspá consisting of dwarf names are then provided to show the lineage of the dwarfs.[12]

People tend to confuse this with the creation of man and often associate one with the other. It is very important to keep a clear distinction in mind, especially since we know[13] that dwarfs are susceptible to light, and that sunlight actually turns them to stone.

Now the ancestry of the Gods seems to flow in parallel. The High explains that Ymir was sustained by the cow named Auðumbla, which was formed just after Ymir, from the drips of the melting rime (it is quite ironic that in English, we have an expression 'Holy Cow' – could it be a surviving reference to this?). From her teats flowed milk which Ymir drank. The cow herself licked the Ice of Niflheim gradually over the span of three days, uncovering from the ice a man named Búri, who was described as large, powerful and beautiful to behold. Búri then married a Jötunn called Bestla (remember, all Jötnar are descended from Ymir). They had three sons: Oðin, Vili and Vé (those three who make the gifts to Ask and Embla), who later on murder Ymir. From the blood flowing out of his body, all Jötnar are drowned except for Bergelmir and his wife, who survived and repopulated the Jötnar race.

Parallels – or rather, points of reference to this – are found in the *Poetic Eddas*, namely the *Völuspá*, *Vafþrúðnismál*, *Grímnismál*, and *Hynduljóð*, which outline how the Gods created the earth, skies, trees and so forth from Ymir's corpse. Important points to remember here are that rime was made of the poisons/toxins originating from Niflheim as they froze – in effect, mixing toxin and water to produce final rime. This is why Ymir is described as 'evil'. (*Vafþrúðnismál* tells of how Ymir is formed of the poison that dripped from the river sources in Niflheim's Élivágar – one of the icy rivers found in that world.)

The final point to look at is Midgard. We learn from the same source that Midgard was the name given to the fortifications created from Ymir's eyebrows. When describing the creation of the earth, the High states that it is circular and around it lies the depths of the seas. The lands along the shores were given to the Jötnar and

15

on the inside was a fortification made called Midgard. The Völuspá[14] attests to that as well. Midgard was given to humans who made it their home.

Let us look briefly at the entire Heimðall issue before delving into what all this actually means. Heimðall is a mysterious God, to say the least. He is son to Nine Mothers, attested to possessing foreknowledge, is all-seeing and hearing and the "whitest of the gods". All these characteristics are important hints as to his actual nature. We encounter him in the Völuspá:

> "Hearing I ask from the holy races,
> From Heimdall's sons, both high and low;
> Thou wilt, Valfather, that well I relate.
> Old tales I remember of men long ago."[15]

The mention here with respect to the sons of Heimðall refers to mankind. Many struggle with the high and low part but there is no difficulty encountered when taken in context with the Rígsmál (Lay of Ríg) and his fathering of the classes of mankind. In the context of the Rígsmál, it is important to notice that this fathering of mankind is an ongoing process: the Thrall's parents are referred to as 'great-grandfather', then we have the Karl's parents as 'grandfather' and finally the Jarls as 'father' and 'mother'. This suggests that his seeding of mankind is a cross-generational ongoing perfecting of the end result, until he reaches the Jarls.

The other important hint as to his nature is to be found in the Þrymskviða:

> "Then Heimdall spake, whitest of the gods,
> Like the Wanes he knew the future well:..."[16]

Here again, the whiteness of the God is emphasised, but

this time so is his ability of foresight, which is compared to that of the Wanes (another term for the Vanir). It is interesting that he appears to be connected to the Vanir, as well as to the Völva (via the Spá[17] training) which is also a Vanir art (the art of prophecy, learned via Seiðr training). His whiteness presents a most amusing dilemma when handled by academics because it is not explained or commented on in other sources – all that is ever mentioned is either that he is the whitest of Gods or the brightest, once again referring to some sort of colouration. It is also fascinating to see how this surfaces in the Rígsmál in terms of inherited genetics. It takes him three attempts to embody himself fully in what were then 'compatible' human beings, before finally producing the Jarl, who embodies his divine potential and capabilities, and to whom he teaches hidden runic mysteries.

In the *Prose Edda*, Heimðall is mentioned in the books *Gylfaginning*, *Skáldskaparmál*, and *Háttatal*. In *Gylfaginning*, the enthroned figure of High tells the disguised mythical king Gangleri of various Gods, and, in chapter 25, the High mentions that Heimðall is known as "the white As" (As here refers to the Æsir), is "great and holy", and that nine maidens, all sisters, gave birth to him. Heimðall is called Hallinskiði and Gullintanni, and he has gold teeth. High continues that Heimðall lives in "a place" called Himinbjörg and that it is near Bifröst. Heimðall is the watchman of the Gods, and he sits on the edge of heaven to guard the Bifröst bridge from the Jötnar.

One fascinating insight we gain is that Heimðall is Loki's enemy and that at Ragnarök, they will kill each other. Energetically speaking, this is extremely insightful – Heimðall, who represents the light and whiteness, battles Loki who represents darkness, and they kill each other. This would in effect indicate the destruction of both pole and anti-pole during the confrontation of these two Gods. Both light and darkness – or their embodiments – get extinguished. But lose not hope: Baldur, who is the Æsir's embodiment of Light, rises from Helheim. A rebirthing of a higher form of Light?

What do we know of Heimðall's mothers? We find very precise information in the *Völuspá hin skamma*:

> "One there was born in the bygone days,
> Of the race of the gods, and great was his might;
> Nine giant women, at the world's edge,
> Once bore the man so might in arms.
> Gjolp there bore him, Greip there bore him,
> Eistla bore him, and Eyrgjafa,
> Ulfrun bore him, and Angeyja,
> Imth and Atla, and Jarnsaxa.
> Strong was he made with the strength of the earth,
> With the ice-cold sea, and the blood of swine."[18]

This identifies him as belonging to the race of Gods with a parenthood of Nine Giantesses. His mother's names are only mentioned in this source, with the exception of Gjolp and Greip, who are also mentioned as being Jötunn maidens, and Jarnsaxa, who is the mother of Thor's son Magni.[19] Hence we have a God who is ranked amongst the Æsir as the brightest and most holy, who is possibly of Vanir heritage, but most certainly of Jöturn heritage, who seeds himself in the human lines and is considered to be the embodiment of whiteness.

Loki said:
> "48. Hush thee, Heimðallr, to a hateful life
> wast doomed in days of yore:
> with a stiff back thou must stand always
> and wake as the watch of the gods."[20]

Oðin and Heimðall are clearly two separate deities, as this stanza directly identifies strife between Oðin and Heimðall with the result being Heimðall's 'punishment' (as it is implied by Loki) to stand watch over the Bifröst Bridge. Each of the referenced poetic translations identifies a 'punishment' imposed upon Heimðall, some with Loki's tone in a more malevolent fashion, but only the Hollander translation specifically identifies Heimðall's 'position' as a charge laid upon him. Considering the only written record of the repercussions of the Vanic War is the chronology of the creation of the holy mead as a bond between them, such a direct reference to Heimðall's 'punishment' (the only legitimate reference to any God or Goddess being punished) is acceptable as evidence of a charge, or duty, levied upon an oppositional leader to a conflict; this is very clear and re-enforces the probability that this duty was imposed, as referred to in the sentence: "wast doomed in the days of yore".

This leaves the human root ancestry as an intricate web of inheritance. We have the original hair from Ymir which brings the heat-imbued water, poisons and frost of Niflheim embodied in the first created Being. They were then forged into tree form by the Gods after they kill Ymir (from his hair) and placed in Midgard, hence forging an intricate relationship between man and Yggdrasil itself. Following that, the three Gods Oðin, Húnir and Lóðurr imbue the original man and woman with their gifts (resulting from a grant of their respective essences), then the Norns grant (or rather 'impose' upon) mankind Ørlǫg and to top it all off, Heimðall imbues some with various degrees of his own essence. Hence you get a mish-mash of original essence from Niflheim, which has passed through certain stages of transformation, to the original evil being (as termed by the High One), then Æsir essence and to top it all off, more Jöturn (this time female) essence and potentially Vanir essence via Heimðall.

This gives human beings an origination older than that of the Gods themselves, and certainly a more intricate one.

Ymir was the original 'evil'. It is important to be careful not to fall into the trap of common definitions of evil when dealing with that term. Here it does not refer to the modern-day understanding of good vs evil, which is utter nonsense, but rather to disruption (or destruction). Remember, the Gods maintain order, and order needs to be disrupted for growth. These disruptions come in the form of opposing often (but not always) destructive forces. These are the forces termed 'evil' in this context. Most would think of it as 'chaos' but to the Norse, chaos meant something very different. It is not until the Victorian period that the definition of chaos became one which is understood today: utter randomness and breaking of all order. We will look at the actual meaning of chaos at a later point in time. In Ymir's context, this disruptive 'evil' is very accurate – his existence sets in motion a massive disruption of the flow of order present at that time. It gives rise to life and creation itself. Trees (through Ymir) are more ancient in heritage than the Gods themselves and through Mjötvið (Yggdrasil), probably even more so.

We know that Búri (the 'root' father) of the Gods was born out of the ice from Niflheim – this is after Ymir was already in existence. This raises an interesting set of questions: were the 'gifts' bestowed on mankind and the imposition of Ørlǫg-Wyrd an attempt to counterbalance Ymir's essence within? To reshape it? If so, what would the combination/unification of the two do? Could this be why we do not express pure essence (in terms of creation) as they do? And why we are prone to complexities? From a universal point of view, it would make sense for the tendency to diversify rules when it comes to attempting to produce unique Beings.

A final fascinating line of enquiry for personal meditation can be found within the fact that Heimðall teaches mankind the runes (see Rígsmál where he teaches them to his sonRíg) rather than Oðin. Oðin leaves snippets of wisdom and guidance on their application but it seems to be Ríg who actually teaches the full scope of their use to the Jarls. As we have seen within these volumes, using the runes is not simply a matter of writing, chanting or bleeding them; you need all the foundational work done before you can effectively unleash a runic power. This is taught by Heimðall (who is of Giant heritage). Oðin, on the other hand, leaves teachings for those who are wise enough to interpret and apply them. This assumes an already existing foundation in terms of runic work. An interesting fact to ponder upon, especially in terms of the light of individual rune streams, which we shall cover at a later point in time (remember, Heimðall is the whitest of Gods!). For the time being, let us return to the subject matter at hand: The Human Being, after a brief look at where, according to the *Eddas*, human beings live.

Insights Into The Nature of Midgard (Earth)

Having looked at the insights provided by the *Eddas* with respect to the creation of the Human Being, it is worth taking a brief look at what insights they can provide us in regards to our home world (Midgard). As children born in Midgard, mankind are subject to its forces, rules and environments, deriving a lot of characteristics and expressing those of his Self through those limitations (in scientific terms, this is called epigenetics and genetics).

In *Alivissmal*[21] (*Poetic Eddas*), Thor and the all-wise dwarf called Alvis speak of many things specifically, Alvis shares his wisdom with relation to the perceptions of inhabitants of the nine worlds. When it comes to Midgard, the encounter unfolds as:

> 9. "Answer me, Alvis! | thou knowest all,
> Dwarf, of the doom of men:
> What call they the earth, | that lies before all,
> In each and every world?"

Alvis spake:
> 10. "Earth to men, Field | to the gods it is,
> The Ways is it called by the Wanes;
> Ever Green by the giants, | The Grower' by elves,
> The Moist by the holy ones high."

Here we see that Midgard is referred to by different names by different species. This is natural and to be expected. We have seen in *The Spirit of Húnir Awakens - Part 1* that everyone's perceptions are totally unique and the commonality in differences is shared across species. Fortunately for us, this gives us deeper insight into the nature of the things discussed. What is meant here is that if you are fortunate enough to know of the labels (and hence perceptive interpretations) of various species of a given common thing, you can get more insight into it than you would simply through your own perception(s).

Here we see that men call it Earth –, that should

necessitate no further explanation. Field is the term the Gods assign to it. Sometimes we have slightly different translations but essentially they all refer to a defined self-standing space of natural setting. In fields, things grow, children play, animals grow and so forth. It is a space for growth. In other words, a space where all the Seeds (Sparks of Self) have a chance to be nourished and to mature. It is interesting to note that the Earth is termed as the 'enclosure' by the Völva in the *Völuspá* (stanza 8). Both terms point to the same underlying concepts – whether you call it a field or an enclosure, it is a defined and kept space for growth. 'The Ways' is the term assigned to it by the Vanir (the Wanes is an anglicised version of this word). This one is a most interesting term, which hints at the very nature of Midgard as the centre point of creation. If you want to get anywhere, you go first to the centre and from there find countless pathways (or ways) to your destination. 'Ever green' is the term the Giants use for the Earth. This is a representation of the cycles of nature on Earth and its ability to sustain life – it is ever green, due to being always flooded with life and living beings. Ever sprouting forth into new life manifestation. The elves call it 'the grower' – in other words, hinted at the fact that Midgard herself is growing and maturing as well as growing all the life on/within her. A most accurate term. This matches yet again with 'The Moist' term used by the holy ones. This is not the time or the space to enter into discussions of the separate yet seldom spoken of species, but just of their perceptions. The Moist yet again suggests an environment for growth – moist earth is after all the ideal growing ground for the Seeds of Yggdrasil! This reference to moist earth has an important connotation of characteristics of the element of earth, the rune ᛟ Óðal (Othala) and the human body itself (which is flesh made moist by blood)! Remember, the principle of 'like attracts like' – our bodies share a likeness with our world.

This concept of seeds is not exclusive to the Norse tradition. We find it prominently featured in many others, including Christianity, with analogies to the garden of Eden and mankind's souls being seeds which were planted and are growing. Those who are curious enough can refer to the relevant biblical texts. For our work, it is time to look at the body, its biological awareness and how we can enhance (as well as make use of) its full potential.

Our Bodies – Our Foundational Seed

In today's 'modern' world, we have a highly destructive relationship with our bodies. The level of mistreatment, even ranging to what could loosely be called 'abuse', disregard, and so forth is staggering. With the advent of modern medicine and changes in attitudes, this disrespect for our very physiology is reaching highly damaging levels. The proof for this is the massive increase in mental and physiological disorders which are mostly the result of friction in-between what can be termed the 'biological awareness' and conscious awareness (think of it as body vs mind, if you prefer).

The body has been subject to much harm over the ages, primarily through religious misconceptions, and secondarily through socially imposed ones, causing it much pain, harm, restrictions and ultimately speaking, damage in all shapes and forms.

Such misunderstanding stems from the fact that it was always perceived as something to be subjugated, controlled, tortured, manipulated or restricted (and the list goes on). In modern times, this has not diminished by any stretch of the imagination. It has become subtler and conflicted but we can still see these patterns present, in many cases in even more dangerous manifestations. Now, in addition to all the harmful practices of the past, we also have chemicals, radiation, poisons, genetically modified food sources, custom-made viruses, the wonders and not so much wonders of modern medicine and let us not forget shame, guilt and rejection.

When looking at the spiritual side of things, we see most if not all religions focus on the body being something 'evil', 'sinful' or simply 'temporary'. Needless to say, all these labels, as well as their significance, is nothing more than illusory due to the fact that they all misinterpret its actual reasons for being. The problem, however, stems from the fact that people judge the body in their limited insight and then push these judgements as facts upon others. If you lack the spiritual maturity to appreciate the significance and purpose of the flesh that is fine, but do not impose it on others and artificially limit theirs as well. The entire 'modern' spiritual view of the body being nothing more than a vehicle or a holographic project is such an example of a deep misunderstanding of a spiritual truth.

It is important to grasp, right from the outset, that the body and the mind – through the Spirit (Óðr) – are directly connected, yet are nonetheless separate parts of the Self. Nothing could illustrate this better than the simple fundamental fact that we have a central nervous system (used by the intelligence of the mind to communicate with the body) and an autonomic nervous system (used by the intelligence of our biology to communicate with our minds). Both of these express a form of intelligence in their own right: the mental intellect (which we are all way too familiar with) and the biological intelligence (which we typically disregard as a matter of course). When the two clash, most people will try to override the biological, be it through medication, through willpower or by simply disregarding it and its attempts to communicate.

You might wonder: so what? Does it matter whether the biological/body side of the Self is listened to or not? Is it not simply a tool for our Spirit (Óðr) used to experience the world? The answer to all these is that yes, it matters, and more so than one could imagine. Why? Simply put, our biological intelligence and awareness is also evolving and it is our fundamental responsibility to help it do so. The other answer is that our evolution is directly dependent on it and its evolution. This might seem an odd concept to the casual onlooker, but those of us who understand these interactions within the Self and within the nervous systems, it becomes a given.

Let us shed a little light on why this is the case. Modern psychology and medicine in general, as well as scientific research, have pretty much got to grips with the fact that mind affects body, and is making good progress in terms of the body affecting the mind. What will be understood at some point in the not-too-distant future is that the body's intelligence and awareness impacts the general intelligence of the human being. Our bodies have a strong impact on the stability, balance and capabilities of our minds (and hence our intellect). We will see later on how, when we bring the two into better synchronicity, our mind and conscious awareness expands beyond its current patterns of function and limitation. The range of possibilities and perceptions suddenly broaden in scope, sometimes in an incredible way. The opposite runs true as well: the more disharmony or the more disjointed these two parts of us become, the greater the difficulties in focus, concentration and perception that will occur. When such disharmonies become severe enough, mental disease and disorders ensure.

Modern-day doctors simply try to deal with this by medicating, which is a way to silence the biological awareness, or rather to stop it from communicating effectively with the mental (the conscious awareness). This is done in order to make you feel better or to stop the disruption in daily life. What it actually does is make the underlying problem much worse, because the wedge being built between mind and body is grown by the simple fact that we are yet again forcing the body to our will, even though it is crying out for help. The most severe interventions where we try to re-wire the mind (think electro-magnetic therapies applied to the brain) or disable the body from communicating with it (think removal of glands and bio-chemical-producing organs such as the endocrine organs) lead to a permanent severance in one of the many natural functions of body-mind communication. Unfortunately, such cases result in more than just making one feel better – it becomes more akin to making one not feel the incoming biological communication in the first place. This we think of as feeling better, due to the lack of disturbing, disruptive or unpleasant sensations or experiences. We literally cripple a part of the Self because we are not able or willing to deal with the underlying issues. As you can imagine, this results in many highly negative consequences for both the body and mind, but also for the entire Self. It is why we need to start learning to work with our biology and the first step to doing so is to build a healthy respect towards the **sanctity of our body**. Stopping this constant violation of the Self just because we can or because we feel like we would be better afterwards is no excuse. We will look at how biological awareness responds to medical and surgical interventions later on. For now, it should be clear that it is initially seen as a violation of the Self, no matter the reason.

The last statement is very harsh indeed, but true nonetheless. Why is this so? Because the biological awareness does not recognise, know or understand reasoning, words or other tools of the intellect. They are all simply mental noise to it that it ignores because they have no significance whatsoever. This is why each time we interact with it in practice, we will have to use sensations to communicate, very much as you did when working with the Hamingja. It is only the mental parts of the Self which understand language or rather derive meaning from it. We have, in today's society, become totally obsessed with words, to the point where we only think in linguistics with only the rarest exceptions. We have already covered just how limiting linguistics are to both the mind and the Self in general, in *The Spirit of Húnir Awakens - Part 1*, so there is no need to repeat it all here. What matters at this point is to understand that the biology does not understand or recognise words. It has its own system of communication, which is pain, pleasure, feelings (in terms of sensations), feelings (in terms of emotions, which are the reaction our minds have to the chemical stimulus generated by the biology), resistance (in terms of physiological tension) and so forth. Learning to communicate with the biological awareness involves becoming aware of these attempts to communicate, acknowledging them and responding to them. The more we do that, the stronger our bond without biology becomes and then, in turn, it reaches more to our minds and tries to help in whatever ways it can. Increased recovery from illness and injury, feeling of being well, contentment within our Self, being happy in our own skin, feeling that life is not a constant battle against countless resistances and so forth are all things to look out for, and a sign that the biological awareness and conscious awareness (body and mind) are becoming more and more synchronised.

Why does this matter for energy work? Or rune mysteries? **The answer is extremely simple: as you unite the two systems of awareness, they both expand to something which is beyond the total capability of each individually. The sum is greater than the combined totality of the parts.** We have talked about individuality, differences and uniqueness in previous publications, and here it is worth mentioning that combined and synchronised, the sum of the two types of awareness – or intelligences, if you prefer – produce manifold multiplication of characteristics, which in turn results in heightened individualisation of the Self. This can only occur when we accept those parts of the Self and work with them, rather than reject them or force them into something they are not. The runic and energetic end result is an incredible growth of potential for both varieties of energies (and runes) and for the expression of those energies and all their variations. Remember, you can only fully master a given force or energy if you can master each and every permutation, no matter how subtle, of that force or energy. This is why we never use the term 'rune master', because it is incorrect to claim oneself a 'rune master', as mastering a rune's forces and subtle infinite permutations would require mastery of the whole range of creation. Let us be brutally honest: this is currently well beyond the reach of any human being. Instead, the focus is to master as many as possible. With the unification or synchronisation of more and more parts of the Self, the range of perception increases and so does the ability to perceive and master further permutations of each and every rune. Once we have mastered all those available to a fully unified Self, we multiply the perfected Self into other realms of possibility to expand once again, and the cycle continues. Even the Gods are still learning, and Oðin himself is a perfect example of that: constantly seeking out new knowledge, new adventures, new possibilities...

The final point to keep in mind, which is by far the most important, is that our body is our foundation. Anyone denying this is simply deluding him or herself. It is the root of our evolution. It gives all the non-shaped bound parts of the Self a shape to work with. In actuality, it dictates our final shape, as all the other parts are formed to be exact replicas of our bodies. Our energy body (Hamr) has exactly the same shape as our physical body (Lik), our shadow body (Sal) takes on a fluidic version that matches that shape, our Hamingja is shaped to the exact replica of our physical, our Fylgja merges into and expands throughout that physical shape, our breath (Önd) flows through the shape (but within its confines), our minds (Hugr) and memory (Minni) shape into our brains' shapes and flow throughout the nervous systems of our entire biology, our Spirit (Óðr) is shaped according to the physical shape and so forth. Our physical body's (Lik) shape is absolutely fundamental to the entire Self. **Think of it in these terms: our body is the crystallisation of our essence and power.** Those who systematically disregard this simple fact fail to mature spiritually and energetically.

All too often, people complain about not being able to project, the body bothering them and so forth. One of the biggest reasons for this is simply due to them not shaping it as an exact replica of their physical shapes.

Put another way, our conscious awareness is used to functioning in our bodies, our biological awareness only knows the shape of our body, learning new shapes, how to perceive from within them, takes dozens of years, learning the subtle impulses, movements, synergies – even the equivalent of producing a heartbeat in a different shape – can take an entire lifetime. Expecting these various awarenesses to just hope out of the familiar territory into a totally alien one (into a new shape) and function normally within is simply foolish.

But wait: what about shapeshifting? The Sagas and Eddas talk about that a lot. Learning to shapeshift requires a vast array of skills and a very significant period of training. Additionally, you need to be able to fully function at all levels of the Self in your CURRENT shape, before even being able to start that learning process. This is the reason why every one of us is not shapeshifting left right and centre. It would be fun, but the amount of investment in terms of energy, resources and time needed would effectively rob us of our time, which is better invested in spiritual evolution and mastery of the runes. Some will argue that they have the ability from past lives, yet again here we come to the misconceptions of past lives in general. Those things which humans label 'past lives' are nothing more than ancestral memories seen and experienced from your own eyes. Transmitted through genetic inheritance, they now, for all intents and purposes, appear as yours by default. Since your mind is unable to distinguish a memory you have from another person as not yours, it will seek out a way to explain it in terms of that memory being 'yours', hence past life recall is a convenient way of doing so. Remember, on the mental level of the Self, there is no space and no time, so an inherited memory – or a memory, for that fact – does not need to be one thing only; it can be an entire lifetime. This is actually the function of the Fylgja, which we will look at in depth at a later point in time.

Time to get back to our very best friend in life: our biological awareness.

The Blood of Lóðurr Awakens

BIOLOGICAL AWARNESS

The Physical Body - Foundation For Biological Awarness

Body awareness is young; our physiological age only reaches about 15 years old in our so-called 'old age'.[22] This means that our bodies never fully mature and what we perceive as a fully mature person and old age are nothing of the sort. It is hard to view a person who is 60 or 70 or older and tell them that their bodies are about 15 years old, but their cellular biology age is exactly that. What this means is that our boiological awareness never matures and is pretty much 'stuck' in childhood from the start to the very end of our lives. The only way to actually mature it and hence realise an awakening of the entire Self is to intervene in this process. It is only by conscious guidance that we can quicken its maturation.

Many have heard the expression of the 'child within' or being in touch with your 'inner child'. What these expressions are actually referring to is this very body awareness. As you consciously connect with it and start working with it, you will notice a lot of childhood wants, behaviours and impulses surfacing in your daily consciousness. The desire to hug someone, to be cared for, looked after, the desire to play, to do childish things, to say or think in childish ways and so forth are all direct manifestations of this biological awareness through your conscious awareness. When this starts to happen, you will know that you have established a strong and stable connection to this biological awareness and can start working with it (see 'Awakening the Bodily Awareness & Intelligence' below).

Cherish it, care for it, and be aware of it. It is a child – a child within in every possible sense, since it seeks attention, it seeks experience, it seeks to be looked after. It will have to learn as much as possible to even given you a small opportunity of maturing it fully. Until it does, neither the energy body (Hamr) nor the shadow (Sal) will become fully active. Yes, they might spontaneously activate for a brief instant or two, but full maturity and hence activity – the breaking out of the energetic shell – can only occur once all these three parts of the Self mature (Lik, Hamr and Sal).

Pay attention to what your body likes and dislikes very closely. You will feel the impulse – some describe it as a pull, others as a soft vibration and others still as a desire emanating from the flesh, whilst some even describe it as an impulse for something or other. These are all valuable insights and hints into what your biological awareness wants and needs at any given point in time. Dislikes are often communicated as the reverse – in other words, as a dislike of something, a not wanting to do something, an aversion out of the blue, a type of nervousness of the body (we have all experienced this one at some point or other, the inability to stand still or focus), or some even report feeling slightly sick, a gut sensation and so forth. These are just some of the ways in which your biological awareness is telling you something is wrong or not wanted. Pay very close attention to these and where possible, try not to override the sensation(s) you receive. The more you do, the more the biological awareness will interpret that as the mind overriding it and you will have the resulting 'pissed off' child to deal with. Here, being the strict parent is not the way to go unless you are 1000% certain of a highly beneficial outcome you can prove to your biological awareness has benefited it. For instance, let us say you are about to go to the gym for the first time or have had a break and your body just does not feel like going back. You are getting all the hallmark signs of a desire to not go. In this case, overriding it and actually going, forcing the body through it will be hard but at the end of the session, it will feel so much better, and will be stronger once it has recovered – so much so that the biological awareness will experience the direct benefit of your mind's overriding the impulse not to go. Additionally, if you then do something as simple as run your hands over your developing body, focus in on the feeling of the muscles, or the feeling of the smaller fat loads and send an intent of 'see how much better we are now', you will be directly communicating that benefit to it. Knowing when to do and when not to do something like this is the hardest lesson you will ever have to learn, but it is well worth the effort. Such experiences will serve to consolidate the relationship you have with your biological awareness.

 Growing this relationship then bolsters your relationship with both the shadow (Sal) and the energy body (Hamr) because this biological awareness is a direct manifestation of the product of theirs. Additionally, for those of you who are planning to have children or already do, it will teach you a whole range of invaluable skills when it comes to parenting. Often new parents complain that they have no skills for being a good parent or that there is no one to teach them. Oh, how wrong they actually are. If they only knew! Parenting the growing Self IS the learning curve. It is the training and skill development for all future parenting.

Parenting aside, this childish biological awareness holds the key to actually manifesting abilities, powers and skills in the energetic (and hence physical) levels of reality – it is the key which unlocks both the energy body (Hamr) and the shadow (Sal). If you see a rune mystic who is always serious, never letting go, you will know that he has not yet fully integrated the whole Self. However, if you encounter one who is serious but at times when interacting with the world displays child-like playfulness, does things because they are fun and laughs about matters, then you will have encountered a true mystic who works with his WHOLE Self. Those are the mystics with actual knowledge and actual power. You would do well to develop this type of approach when dealing with Creation. Yes, it is serious business but you also have to have fun and most importantly, laugh at things. Always let the inner child loose but have your mind (Hugr) there with its watchful eye, ready to interfere when the need arises. The more your inner child gets to experience things, the more it will mature. Eventually, it will grow and then the REAL fun begins!

In some it might manifest as the beast within. That is the nature of all those who identify with an animalistic Self rather than a childhood one. Let us get one thing straight from the get go: there is absolutely nothing wrong with having a Self rooted in the animalistic (in the Norse tradition it is common both in legend and in the modern day – those are the natural shapeshifters!). Exactly the same rules apply, and actually, those with the animalistic side to the Self find it far easier to grow it than those with the childlike one. In either case, they need to be allowed to 'play' to experience and to be guided in order to grow. Those individuals who exhibit the animalistic Self are far more connected to the natural world and can be very passionate and intense, but they too have the same needs. Such individuals grow best in the presence of another to guide them and safeguard them when the animalistic Self is exploring, whereas those with the childhood Self need to be very disciplined in their own conscious to steer the child within them by themselves. That level of forced maturity is not needed for those of the animalistic Self – they tend to roam 'free' or in the company of another who provides the needed discipline/guidance.

- THE BLOOD OF LÓÐURR AWAKENS -

Body Awareness
Biological Awareness

This expresses itself in one of two ways, depending on the individual: the inner child or the inner beast. These manifestations are set for life and cannot be changed; they depend entirely on you as an individual. The former can be wild as well, and the latter can be your greatest friend and protector. It is important to realise the type of biological awareness you have, to accept it and work with it. What you should avoid doing at ANY cost is trying to judge it or classify one as better than the other. This is being judgmental and imposing human social conditioning on something which is so fundamentally biological that it surpasses all such judgements.

The biological awareness connects to the conscious awareness through the nervous system. The physical body (Lik), being the great foundation and integrator, has not evolved into a dual-nervous system structure randomly – far from it. The central nervous system and the autonomic nervous systems are separate yet interconnected (and highly hierarchical) for a good reason. They represent the two different types of awareness, each with its own consciousness. The former we call conscious and the latter we call subconscious or unconscious – it is truly neither of those, but those concepts are good enough to guide your thinking to it. For some reason, it seems incredibly difficult for 'modern' people to conceive of another type of consciousness within them operating outside of their awareness or control. Baffling...

A quick note here. Before anyone tries to take these concepts and twist them, the beast and child modes of the biological awareness ARE NOT a result of race or gender or anything like this. Do NOT go assuming this to be the case. There is infinite variety, and that includes infinite combinations of those who function along the lines of the one or the other. It is most unwise to assume that the one is better than the other or vice versa.

In our highly primitive approach to dealing with the Self, especially the biological self, rather than allow its own awareness to surface and take control from time to time in order to experience and grow, mankind tends to go all judgmental and tries to override it, over and over again, until eventually at some point or other, control is lost and the child within goes on a rampage or the beast within goes berserk (hint! hint!) and great damage is done. It is far better to allow these inner impulses to be satisfied in an understanding and non-destructive manner under the supervision of the conscious mind. This cycle has been perpetuated for ages, and in the past it was given labels such as possession by 'evil', 'devils', 'demons' and so forth, whereas in fact it was nothing more than the biological awareness finally overwhelming the conscious controls and restrictions and going on a rampage, due to never being allowed to experience what it needs to grow. These days, we see it yet again in all these so-called mental disorders swarming the population. Mankind is being pushed to evolve and that means so is his or her biological awareness. Restrict it, and that very push – which it will feel and experience millions of times more directly and potently than our conscious mind – will cause it to go haywire. Remember, this biological awareness has DIRECT access to all systems in our bodies, including the chemical, biological, neural, genetic and so forth! It can do whatever it wills or feels it needs to short-circuit the Spirit (hence conscious awareness) in whatever way it finds best.

    Why turn your own biology against yourself? It is here for us to experience growth and to evolve with us. Making it an enemy as mankind is doing *en masse* is the road to madness and failure.

- THE BLOOD OF LÓÐURR AWAKENS -

Functions of Biological Awareness

You might be wondering what exactly the purpose of this biological awareness is, and why you need to bother with it. The answer is simple; it is the basis of our complete awareness. This might be a little confusing as a statement, so let us put it into more familiar terminology: you have consciousness, awareness, what people call 'subconscious' or 'unconscious' (basically that other mind which process sensory and information without our conscious mind's involvement), and what we call hyper-consciousness (when your consciousness functions at much higher levels of existence, such as when perceiving directly from energy (see *The Spirit of Húnir Awakens – Parts 1 & 2*). In human beings, all these modes of consciousness and awareness (and hence perception) are separate. We only have access to them whilst they are functional and even then, they might elude us completely. Because the basis of the human being is the physical (or condensed energy, if you prefer), that is our starting point. It is from where consciousness in all humans arises. Biological awareness is not only the link between the Spirit (Óðr) and physical body (Lik), but is the key to both the energy body (Hamr) and the shadow (Sal). By maturing and growing it, we also gain direct experience and perceptions of the entire energy level of reality (and Self). This in turn gives us full access to the all-elusive ability of our Self, which is 'intending'.

Taking this concept a step further, if you look at the whole Self and its nine-fold structure, you will see that the physical body (Lik) is a central point of it. By awakening our conscious harmonisation (and hence integrating) with our biological awareness, we expand our (conscious) awareness into the energy body (Hamr) and shadow (Sal) as well. This achieves a unification of the three parts of our Self at the energetic level, and links them directly with the Spirit (Óðr). Because the Spirit (Óðr) manifests as mind (Hugr) and memory (Minni), those are already integrated and within our conscious reach. Hence we now have the mental/spiritual level of the Self fully integrated with the energetic. Six parts of the Self work in union. In *The Breath of Oðin Awakens*, we saw how the breath (Önd) is made to flow through our DNA and blood, and that this pulled Megin-charged breath into the biological awareness. We learnt to expand the Hamingja throughout the physical body (Lik) which in turn introduced it to the biological awareness, and since the Fylgja (inherited/ancestral spirit) is bound to us at birth, that flows through it as well, via the DNA. As you can see, those latter three brought the archetypal parts of the Self into the flesh. Then we brought more and more of the mental level and now we finally awaken the flesh itself and bring in the energy body (Hamr) and shadow (Sal): this completely unifies ALL the parts of the Self and initiates its harmonisation. Full harmonisation takes time and persistence but the key 'introductions' are all made and these parts of the Self start to exchange information, energy, power, experiences and so forth. The result? A growth in the whole Self, a crossing over of all the levels of Creation within the Self. Slowly, step by step, you become more and more a central point in your own Creation. Your awareness expands and so does your influence (as well as your stability!).

This, ladies and gents, is why the Biological Awareness is such an important part of our Self. It is the foundation into which we ground ALL other parts of the Self and start their unification: we become WHOLE. It is only from this point of being that we can start to get to know our true Self, what and who we are. It is also from this point that we can start to influence life and creation. It is at this point that the Spark of Self can become a Flame of Self capable of radiating its own uniqueness throughout the ENTIRE Self and eventually into Creation itself.

The golden rule is to always give the body what it strives for, its own cellular intelligence also NEEDS to grow, just as our minds do. But wait sometimes the desires of the body cannot be fulfilled – for instance, when things it would want lead to breaking the laws of the land. Yes, that is correct: it is possible, due to the fact that we live in an overly legalistic and politically correct social system. In these cases, there is no point in getting into trouble; simply sending out an intent to the body fused with the reasons why (it is impossible to do without causing it even more harm, such as being in jail, for instance) will suffice. What typically happens in these cases is that after sufficient 'pressure' from such impossibilities of experience and the growth of the biological need for those experiences, the innate cellular biology will start to pull on other resources it has access to which by default, we do not, in order to satisfy those experiential needs. These primarily are the physiological energy systems, the energy body (Hamr) and the shadow body (Sal). It is directly linked to them – more so than our conscious awareness could ever be. As such, it can force them into active functioning in order to displace awareness to another realm of possibilities, in order to gain that experiential knowledge and energy it needs for growth. When the mind and body are in harmony, this type of bypassing of the human limited realms in Midgard can occur smoothly, as the cellular intelligence will know that our awareness can carry those experiences (well their knowledge/informative parts) via memory (Minni) back to it, and the energy body (Hamr) and/or shadow (Sal) can carry the energetic ones. This is why harmony of body and mind is so vitally important. **The mind stirs the physicality into a new range of possibilities and that physically forces the mind to experience them.** Ultimately, it benefits both mind and body; each one grows, hence the Spirit and Flesh evolve in synchronicity.

If your biological awareness is told about the extraordinary and that it cannot access it, it will awaken the energy body (Hamr) or Shadow Self (Sal) to gain access. Once the energy body (Hamr) and shadow (Sal) have experienced them, those experiential energies are brought back to boost the cellular awareness.

Awakening the Bodily Awareness & Intelligence

Awakening might be a somewhat misleading term to use, since the body is always awake – or you would be not only dead, but decomposed. What we are instead achieving is a type of awakening of conscious awareness to the biological one. We are seeking to bring the two closer together and allow your conscious mind to communicate and connect with the body. In order to do so, they need to know each other!

To get started, you will first have to master the 'Shaping the Óðr' practice.[23] It is essential in many practices. If you have not, you should do so. Without it, you will not be able to proceed much further.

What you are going to be doing is reshaping your Spirit (Óðr) into the shape of every organ of your body as follows:

Lungs
Anus
Right eye
Left eye

Stomach
Right ear
Left ear
Whole spine
Left hand
Right hand
Right arm
Left arm
Left leg
Right leg
Left kidney
Right kidney
Diaphragm
Spleen
Abdomen
Liver
Throat
Testicles/ovaries
Right side of nose
Left side of nose
Gallbladder
Brain
Pancreas
Whole gut (Colon + small intestine + appendix)
Heart
Bladder
Urethra
Women: ovaries (inside the lower abdomen, one on the left, the other on the right)
Men: Penis and testicles
Women: Vagina
Women: Clitoris
Women: Womb (VERY IMPORTANT)
Men: Prostate gland (found just above the inside of the anus and midpoint up the urethra)
Adrenal glands (found at the top of each kidney)
Thyroid gland (gland in two parts in front of the windpipe)
Hypothalamus (just above the pituitary gland and optic chiasm, also straight behind the nose)
Thymus

In working the brain, you will start with the whole brain, then do the same with the following subdivisions:

    Left side of brain only
    Right side of the brain only
    Frontal cortex only
    Corpus colostrum (the thick nerve strip running from the top view of the brain from left to right)
    Cerebellum (small brain at the back of head)
    Pineal gland (mid-cranium, straight behind nose)
    Pituitary gland (base of the brain)
    Brain stem (where spine and brain connect)

Then you will reshape into the following:

    Skeleton/bones
    Spine
    Nervous system (autonomous – body nervous system, not brain)
    Brain nervous system

If you are unsure where a given organ is in your body, time to go and look it up. There is ample literature available and quite a few good references with detailed imagery online to refer to.

With the reshaping into nervous systems, you will just need to follow your bodily awareness and intuition because there are countless subtle variations in how individual nerves flow, connect and wrap in each and every one of us. It is impossible to capture them all in illustrations. By the time you reach working with the nervous system, the biological awareness will be aware of what you are doing and assist you.

Having done all of these, you will then proceed to do the same with the muscles in your body, and finally the skin (do not neglect the skin!).

With each of these reshapings, the process is exactly the same in terms of steps:

1. You reshape the Spirit (Óðr) to match the organ/body system.
2. You intend to be it. You feel yourself as it.
3. You then try to perceive its immediate environment. For instance, if you are the liver during your practice, what is happening around the liver on the outside? What fluids are coming into it? What is it sending out? How is it responding and to what is it responding? And so forth. This is a sensory practice where you feel/sense, NOT an intellectual one.
4. Your meditation has to be so deep that you become the liver. You have its shape and you are gaining insight into its purpose and functions. Do not try to interfere with ANY of them. Instead, just observe and experience; query them.
5. Once you have achieved a good union with the liver, intend to be at one with it.
6. Feel it, feel what it is like to be the liver, totally unify with it.
7. Bask in that unity.
8. Then reflect on how it is doing all that it needs to do. Intend to connect with the millions upon millions of liver cells. Acknowledge them, feel them, observe just how much intelligence each and every one of them holds on its own and how they all hold together as 'the liver'.
9. Next, intend yourself (as conscious awareness now united with the liver), to merge with that of the liver cells individually and as a whole. You are becoming part of them and they of you.

Take this step slowly and be thorough with it.
10 Just before you are about to end, it is optional, but definitely worth doing, to send out a sensation of 'thank you' or a sense of gratitude. It is after all thanks to each of the cells and organs as a whole that you are alive and thinking and doing!
11 When you are ready to end, simply reshape the Spirit (Óðr) back into that of your entire body and refocus on becoming at one with the whole body (Lik).
12 You need to feel each organ and unite with it exactly as it is.

Some people will have undergone various surgeries and some might even not have a 'whole' organ or it might be diseased. With these practices, you will notice a gap in the biological awareness and quite often a sense of blame from that awareness directed at you. This is something you are going to have work through. It is impossible to fill the gaps but it is possible to fix the sense of friction or blame an organ's awareness can have with your conscious mind. It is natural it will blame you. If you were born with a health issue or gained it during your youth or as a result of environmental factors, you will not sense any blame but more of a call for help. Remember, you are responsible for it. Communicate with it. As soon as you have completed one organ/system, move onto the next until you complete them all.

When you are communicating with it, it is important to avoid using words. They have absolutely no meaning to your biology. Use sensing and feeling, or pure thought (see *The Spirit of Húnir Awakens – Part 2*), or even better, use both. Remember, here we are, not looking at healing anything, simply we are connecting with and learning about all the parts of our own inner universe at the physical manifestation of the energetic level of our Self.

These practices serve a twofold purpose: the first is connecting with the biological awareness one step at a time and the second is gaining skill in projection of awareness. It is much easier to project and maintain that new locale within your Self than it is without – hence we always start by dealing with the inner physical, which is the most familiar, then move onto the inner pure energetic and finally step out to the outer.

Having done all of these, the final steps involve reshaping into the:

> Cerebrospinal fluid (found flowing throughout the spine up into the brain)
> The lymph system
> The blood system (master this one well; it will be used extensively in the 'Blood – Crystallised Megin and Life Essence' section below).
> The respiratory system

With these, what you do is reshape yourself into the system itself through which these substances flow. Let us take the blood, for example. Here, you take on the shape of veins and arteries, and feel the flow of blood through them as outlined in the practice above. The second step involves spilling your Spirit (Óðr) into the blood itself. In this shaping, you are the blood flowing through the system you just experienced being in the previous step. Note: here we are not shaping into the heart; that was done in the organ reshaping. Instead, you are reshaping into the arteries used by the heart and feeling the blood pumping through you.

Last but most certainly not least, and probably one of the most important parts of this practice, you will need to reshape into the spaces in between, within your physiology. This is a tricky one to do but the greatest effort should be made to master it. Here we are talking about the spaces in between nerves, the spaces in between bones, the spaces in between cells, the pores in your skin where the spaces between skin cells are found and so forth. Getting this right takes time and requires a relatively solid biological awareness working with you. Whatever you do, do not skip this. It is an essential prerequisite for the work you will be doing with your Shadow Self (Sal). Unless this is done, there is no work possible with the Shadow Self (Sal).

Doing these serves as a precursor to building or rather shaping the energy body (Hamr) which is very much misunderstood. It is typically thought of as the blueprint for the physical – in fact, it is a blueprint but not only for the physical, which also has the DNA and epigenetics as well as environmental factors to shape it. The energy body (Hamr) is the blueprint built from the physical, which ultimately evolves into becoming the blueprint for the entire Self. We will look at this in more detail in a later section.

The Blood of Lóðurr Awakens

Expanding
Biological Awareness

This expands on the previous practice. Once you have gained a certain degree of harmony and unity with your body's awareness, you can start to work with it. One key fact to keep in mind is that you are teaching a child. It is the child part of you, so be patient and take things from the point of view of having fun. The more fun and game-like your presentation of what you want it to do, the better results you will have.

You are going to start off by teaching the biological awareness to respond to your needs under conscious direction. This is a big step for it, so be patient and avoid getting frustrated if it fails the first few times. You are literally teaching a baby to walk.

Start off by going into a light trance. This should by now be pretty simple to do. You will do something similar to what you did during the 'Awakening the Biological Awareness' practice above. But instead of reshaping into a given organ, you will reshape into the entire physical shape. Avoid getting confused – yes, this is the usual shape, but the very act of reshaping back into your own shape will bring your conscious and biological awareness into synchronicity. All you need to do is intend to expand out of the head (which is the usual resting place of your consciousness) down throughout the body. As you do so, adopt its shape. You should not only focus on the outer layers of your body, but also become aware of all the organs and inner structures of your physiology as you expand through it. This should be a very simple matter, providing that you have completed the previous practices.

Once you have expanded throughout the entire body, will yourself to feel it from the inside out. Be conscious and sense each and every fibre in your body. Doing so, you will start to feel the awareness flowing out of each and every cell within it. The entire collective of all of these as a uniform oneness is the biological awareness of your body (Lik). This is what you will be working with. We will refer to this simply as the biological awareness from this point onwards.

Unite with it, let your mind flow through it, acknowledge it with respect and feel at one with it. You are ONE. You should notice an echo from it, a type of sense saying 'we are one'. Once you have this, you are ready to proceed. If you do not, simply enjoy sensing it until it manifests. Should it fail to 'click', simply allow a sense of gratitude for its life-maintaining efforts and pull back towards your brain. Once your consciousness is back, chant the ᛗ Maður (Mannaz) rune, feel and see its red soft energy, willing it to harmonise all the parts of your Self. Then use the ᛟ Óðal (Othala) rune, flooding your flesh with its heavy dark yellow energy, feeling it anchoring your Self within it. Repeat on a regular basis until the response comes through. It can take some time, depending entirely on your previous work with the practices above and how good a relationship you have with your body. If need be, repeat the awakening practices to consolidate things further.

Having reached and united with your biological awareness, the next step involves trying to stretch it outwards, only by an inch or so at most. There is no need to push it out further; it can be very harmful to overstretch too fast. All you want to achieve is a shift from its usual position in the cells of your body to just slightly away from them and back, never forgetting to bring it back into the cells fully. With your awareness merged with the biological counterpart, intend it to stretch out by at most one inch in all directions. You are pushing that awareness into the auric field for the first time ever. Allow it to float around the skin and intend it to pull back into its usual resting place.

Before ending the practice, send your biological awareness a sense of achievement – of pride, if need be.

Quick Steps

1 Enter into a relaxed state or light trance.
2 You will need to use the reshaping skills just developed (see above) and reshape into the exact same shape as your physical body (Lik). This will synchronise the conscious and biology. Expand your sense of self out of the head region throughout the entire body.
3 When reshaping, become aware of all the organs and biological systems within your body. Sense every fibre, feel every pulse, each heartbeat and so forth. Become one with your body.
4 Having established a clear sensing of the

biology, intend to feel its awareness. This should result in a shift and response (providing you have expanded throughout everything correctly). Unite with this awareness. Be at one with it. Acknowledge it and show respect for it.

5   Wait to see if the sense of 'we are one' is echoed back to you. If not, rinse and repeat until you get a response. Do not try to force it! Relax and be patient.

6   Providing the connection has been acknowledged by your biology, chant the ᛘ Maður (Mannaz) rune, feeling its soft light red energy harmonising all the parts of your Self. Follow this with the ᛟ Óðal (Othala) rune, sensing its heavier dark yellow energy, anchoring your Self in the flesh (in your biology).

7   Having established the connection and become familiar with it, make sure you are as perfectly united with it as possible, then stretch it outwards. Just by an inch in all directions. Feel yourself and it reaching out of the skin for the first time.

8   Enjoy the sensation and when done, pull it back within the confines of the skin.

9   Send a sense of achievement to the biological awareness and gradually return to your daily activities.

10   Repeat as often as possible until you can achieve this connection instantly whenever needed.

Óðr Merging Into Biological Awareness

This is an extension of the previous practice. Here you are not only merging your awareness, but the full Spirit (Óðr) with the biological awareness. In this case, it will also merge with the biological intelligence. Proceed with the previous practice by stretching out the biological awareness to the one inch outwards. As you do so, hold it there. Switch your mental focus into the Spirit (Óðr).[24] Next, expand the Spirit (Óðr) to match the shape of the biological awareness. In other words, the flow of it will have to be matched by the flowing of the Spirit (Óðr).

Having synched those two up, intend them to merge. This is done by having the Spirit (Óðr) flow through the biological awareness whilst sending out the sense of union coursing through the two. As the two merge, you will also experience this merging through your actual awareness.

Practice this very often because it is vitally important. What we are achieving here is a merging of the biology with the Spirit (Óðr). Spirit (Óðr) and Matter are united and at one with each other. The achievement of this is one of the reasons for life in the flesh.

Runic Flow Into The Biological Awareness

When you have a good unity of the Spirit (Óðr), your conscious and the biological awareness, you are ready to proceed. You will now reshape the Spirit (Óðr) into one of the runes. Select the rune you are most familiar with and work easiest with. That will also be the rune your biological awareness will be the most receptive of. All you need to do is reshape the Spirit (Óðr) into the rune's shape and meditate on being that rune and runestream. Allow the energy to gently expand into the biological awareness by about one inch. Here, the keyword is GENTLY. If at any point you sense resistance, reluctance or a pulling back of the biological awareness, pull back the runic energy IMMEDIATELY and end the practice. Even the slightest hesitation by the biological awareness is enough to take immediate action. At no point whatsoever should you ever, EVER consider forcing this. You have been warned!

When ready to end the practice, simply pull back the runic energy into your Spirit (Óðr) (which is rune shaped) and reshape it to the usual shape of your body. Then send a sensation of achievement or pride or success to your biological awareness as you pull it back into the body (remember, it is still at the one-inch expanded state).

Quick Steps

1 Select a rune you are familiar with and work very easily with.
2 Reshape your Spirit (Óðr) into the shape of that rune (see 'Óðr Shaping into Runes'[25]).
3 Meditate on being that rune, on how you ARE the rune and its runestream of energy.
4 As the energy of the rune (now you) expands outwards, let it flood your biological awareness and flow outwards by an inch. In case of any discomfort, resistance or hesitation, STOP and end the practice for the time being. DO NOT force the biological awareness under

ANY circumstance, it is not worth the fallout.
5   When done, pull back the runic energy into yourself (you are the rune, remember) until it is no more. Then reshape your Spirit (Óðr) into the same shape as your physical body (Lik) and end the practice. You can send through a sense of achievement to your biological awareness, if need be.

Here, no specific runic order is given to work from. This is for two main reasons, one being that the rune(s) you get on best with might be completely different from someone else's. The other is that by thinking a specific rune and sending a query sensation to the biological awareness, you will be able to gauge its response to that rune. In order to do so, simply observe how your body feels, including any reactions and impulses after sending the 'this one?' sensation (or pure thought) to it. By this stage of the practices, you should be sufficiently in tune with it to be able to directly communicate in this manner. Just remember to work through all the runes and not exclude certain ones or overwork others. These practices are artificially evolving the biology in both awareness and intellect as well as energetic terms. Pay special attention to the ᛟ Óðal (Othala) rune – it is the rune of the physical body (Lik). Men will find this easy to do, whereas women will need a little more work and effort due to the ᛟ Óðal (Othala) rune not being anchored in their genetics (it is in the male Y-chromosome).

- THE BLOOD OF LÓÐURR AWAKENS -

Activating Spiritual Biological Awareness

This is something which can only be done whilst we have actual physical bodies. It is one of the main reasons why Spirit (Óðr) enters into matter (in this case, flesh). You are still working at the biological awareness level – that does not change – but you are going to be pushing it a step into and towards the spiritual, in effect forcing its energetic components (remember, matter is condensed (or materialised) energy, after all) to become subtler and hence more akin to rune energy, rather than the dense energy of matter.

There is a very powerful reason for doing this. It will not only allow us to form the outer boundaries of the Óðrerir (Norse 'Holy Grail') but will also awaken the physical to the energetic side of our reality. This is a necessary step to ensuring that you can take it with you post-death, rather than allowing the death process to simply dissolve and decay it all. Yes, a fully formed Self takes its physicality, its Midgard point, with it post-death. It is far too important to leave behind.

This practice requires you to have established the Inner Boundaries of the Óðrerir.[26] The Inner Boundary practice must have been fully mastered, not only with proficiency but with repeated practice. Here, what matters is not only how well you do it but also how often you do.

Stage II: Forming the Óðrerir Outer Boundaries

Now the real fun begins. This builds on the 'Entering into Runic Trance: Strengthening Óðrerir Inner Boundaries' practices.[27] Once you have established the Outer Boundary of the Óðrerir, you will be taking your Mead creation and transformational abilities to a whole new level. Stage II is done in two steps. This is the first one we will cover, and the second one after our discussions of the energy body (Hamr) and shadow (Sal) below. What you are doing in stages I, II and III is establishing the tools of inner alchemy. What follows later on is the actual use of them. In this particular practice, you will be further bridging the spiritual and the physical initially established during the Inner Boundary building.

You need to start by doing the practice of establishing the Inner Boundary.[28] During that practice, when you are instructed to use a rune in order to establish a Runic Mead, use the ᛟ Óðal (Othala) rune. Hold onto that energy – in other words, do not send it over into the Hamingja as directed. We will be doing something a little different with it here.

ᛟ Óðal (Othala) is the runic energy which has the strongest effect(s) on the physical (Lik). It is, after all, our 'home' during life. Whether you like it, hate it, think it is great or awful does not change that core basic fact. Deal with your issues and harmonise with your spiritual home (the physical body (Lik)).

Assuming you have done the Inner Boundary practice correctly, you should be at a point where you have the mind (Hugr) and Spirit (Óðr) forming the blue-ish glowing boundaries extending about half to one inch around your physical (Lik). The next step is a type of bridging of that initial Óðrerir deeper into manifestation using your physical body (Lik). The trick to doing so is to become aware of your biological awareness as you did in the previous practices. This time, rather than merging the Spirit (Óðr) with it, you are going to send out an intent to your biological awareness to merge into the Spirit (Óðr). Be careful here: it is in the driving seat, so it might merge, or it might refuse. Respect its decision. If it refuses, end the practice and try another time. Do not feel disappointment or hold a grudge or be angry. That will just make matters worse in the long term. Remember, it has far deeper knowledge of what you are doing than you do and there might be a very good reason why it decides the time is not now, that it is not ready or even that you are not ready. It will put stops into your work in order to protect you, if need be.

Assuming it does respond to your intent, guide it to flow around the shape you have established, for the Inner Boundary of the Óðrerir. Biological awareness loves to wrap itself from the outside in, whereas Spirit (Óðr) does the opposite and flows from the inside out. We are naturally going to be using both modi operandi. Guide or follow the biological awareness as it flows out and around your shaped Óðrerir. It will eventually form a type of skin on it and settle down. As it does, allow the ᛟ Óðal (Othala) runic energy you build up during the runic trance to flow outwards: towards it. Take this VERY SLOWLY and steadily. Allow the biological awareness to accept it. When it does, the awareness will start to pull onto it. Just observe; do not interfere or try to guide this process, you will make a mess of it if you do. Eventually, your biological awareness will pull on all of the ᛟ Óðal (Othala) Mead energy and merge it into itself. This will do a few fascinating things spontaneously. It has a type of 'glue' effect where it coalesces the biological awareness with the Óðrerir and causes the former to fully seal the outer boundaries. You will then notice that it not only remains on the boundaries like a skin – that of course, does remain – but it also expands inwards, eventually bringing that solidity to the entire Óðrerir shape you have established. Some parts of it even connect to the centre point within the Óðrerir. You might or you might not notice this. Whether you do or not is irrelevant at this point; I am just mentioning it in case you do and wonder what is happening.

With this, you have established both the Inner and Outer Boundaries of your Óðrerir. This is a significant step in the formation of your Self. Enjoy it.

If you wish, you can now proceed to doing the Runic Trance practice in order to form a far more solid (and hence tangible) version of the Runic Meads than you did previously when working with only with the Inner boundaries.

To end this practice, you will take a few different steps than you would with typical practices. Here, you will send any energy you have produced (Runic Meads) into the Hamingja. As with working with just the Inner boundary, you are not going to dissipate ANY of it, because that would result in a weakening of the Self. You want the opposite – a strengthening. Now, since you have the biological awareness merged within the Óðrerir to end the practice, you need to intend that awareness to stretch itself back into the physical body (Lik). You can see why those practices to stretch it were important to master above. This is a necessary step because that biological awareness makes each and every cell of your body function. We need it there, not just in the Óðrerir. Since it has a natural tendency of flowing inwards and your Óðrerir's shape contains the physical body (Lik) within itself this stretching inwards is a completely natural thing for it to do and should present no problem whatsoever.

Quick Steps

1 Start by establishing the Inner Boundaries of your Óðrerir.

2 During the establishing of the Inner Boundaries, use the ᛟ Óðal (Othala) runic energy to create your Runic Mead. Hold onto that energy rather than sending it to the Hamingja.

3 With the Inner Boundary established, you should have the mind (Hugr) and Spirit (Óðr) forming the blue-ish glowing boundary at about half to one inch around your physical body (Lik). Become aware of your biological awareness (connect with it) and intend it to merge with the Spirit. Remember, here it is in the driving seat. It might, it might not or it might simply refuse to respond. Respect its decision. It is not yours to make, it is entirely down to your biological awareness here.

4. Assuming that it accepts your request and responds, guide it to wrap itself from the outside in. What you get is the biological awareness merged with the blue-ish energy pulsating from the inside out and the biological awareness pulsating from the outside in. It is guided to form a type of skin around your Óðrerir's shape (its Inner Boundary).
5. Once your outer layer is in place (the biological awareness) which is wrapping the inner (that blue-ish glow), allow the ᛟ Óðal (Othala) Runic Mead you kept hold off to flow outwards towards the biological awareness (which is like a second skin, now that it has settled down). Providing that awareness accepts it, it will start to pull on it, as the ᛟ Óðal (Othala) energy is very familiar to it (for both genders!). Do not try to guide this process or interfere with it.
6. When it has finished absorbing this ᛟ Óðal (Othala) Runic Mead, it will coalesce, causing a type of tightening around the inner layers of the Óðrerir and binding itself with them.
7. To end the practice, you simply have to get the biological awareness to extend itself back throughout the entire physical body (Lik).

When you do this the first few times, the stretching will make cracks in your Óðrerir as it pulls back into the physical. This is unavoidable and part of the building of the Outer Boundaries process. The more often you do this, the more your Óðrerir will become accustomed to it and to being within the physical, and at the same time, fewer and fewer cracks will remain. Eventually, it will not allow any to remain. With regular practice, you will also be not only stretching but enhancing the volume of this awareness to the point where there will be so much of it that it will outstrip the amount of cells it can inhabit. It then naturally shifts into the Óðrerir as its second 'home'. You can enhance this process and its related effects by producing Runic Mead from the ᚢ Úr (Uruz) rune and the ᛚ Lögur (Laguz) rune.

The Blood of Lóðurr Awakens

BIOLOGICAL AWARENESS
BACK TO BASICS

Overview of Enhancement

We have seen how to make use of biological awareness, or at least how to master our first few steps in that direction. When dealing with the physical body (Lik) in our physical reality, it is necessary to bring the two into focus, otherwise all the things we do on a daily basis will have a significant impact without you being even aware of it. Most notably, we are going to look at how things we commonly interact with affect it: food, exercise, stress and so forth. Naturally, it is impossible to look at each and every one in complete detail – that would be impractical – but enough information can be given to guide you in the proper direction.

Body Types

Many people try and pursue a healthier lifestyle for the sake of well-being and longevity. Others do not care much about it at all and seek to enjoy life as much as they possibly can, irrespective of what may happen down the line. Each to his or her own. However, a rune mystic cannot afford such a luxury (nor can anyone else seeking to work with energy or what could be loosely called that beyond the usual daily work, friends, shopping, TV and gossiping cyclic routine human beings enjoy so much).

For us, health is absolutely paramount due to the fact that any physiological impairment we might have will reduce our energy perception and use abilities, and will cause the Megin to flow in order to heal/maintain the body. It will also weaken our general energy reserves which are already extremely minimal, as is the case for any human Being, irrespective of health status quo. When the physical body (Lik) is in distress, this further disrupts the inner balance and harmony we need, and then our biology sees our minds and Self as an opponent against which it needs to work. This leads to all sorts of additional complications which wreck our entire energy system. Such problems then cause the energy body (Hamr) and shadow Self (Sal) to be immensely weakened. Remember, they gain energy from the excess the physical accumulates! It also makes concentration difficult and keeps the mind hindered from achieving the silencing needed for so much. With all these parts of Self out of order (literally), there is no power for intending. This effectively removes the key to achieving anything with energy, no matter how powerful or knowledgeable you might have become. Naturally, once you have moved beyond the limitation of the physical being your only foundation, and you have an active biological awareness in your energy body and/or shadow Self, when the physical weakens, it does not disrupt things to such a degree (if at all). But in order to get to that stage, you need as perfect health as possible.

We have looked at how our physiological organs have specific energy functions. These will not be able to function if the physical body (Lik) is making use of the energy to repair or work around a defect of some sort. If you have a long-term condition, the only way to counter it is to increase the amount of energy you take in to make up for the loss. The more conditions and the greater their physiological impact, the greater that energy will have to be. Very long-term conditions usually rewire the body to some extent and the energy body (Hamr) to a greater one. This means you might have to manually rewire part of the energy systems in order to re-establish proper 'wiring' and stop the harmful or debilitating ones.

Learning to Shape via Physical Body

Shaping is an essential skill for all life forms and this is where the physical body (Lik) comes into play for humanity. Not only does it force us into living in a reality of countless shapes which can be observed and manipulated objectively (as in outside of the Self), but it also teaches us how to reshape those shapes, and to manipulate them and the laws governing them. Midgard and the physical universes as a whole provide a very unique perspective to shape and form and it is this: they all express shape subject to time. This is totally unique to the physical (which, let us remember, is just the densest form of energy). When working on subtler levels of energy, you also experience shape but in a more fluid and timeless manner. It is only once you gain sufficient density of energy that matter arises, which in turn gives rise to the effects of time. Time does not need to always flow in the manner in which we are used to here – it can speed up, slow down and even become erratic but it is present nonetheless. This learning gives the rest of your Self the ability to solidify, if you persistently and diligently work on developing the Self, and eventually no longer have the need for a physical body (Lik) or to be more accurate, a less physical body (Lik) than your current one.

Other than the physical body (Lik), the other parts of our Self are either shapeless per se, have a very basic shape or a fluid one. For instance, our energy body (Hamr) is a basic sphere shape (or an egg in some people), our shadow body (Sal) is an outline into and out of which substance flows along a thin borderline, our Spirit (Óðr) is totally shapeless, our mind (Hugr) and memory (Minni) are also essentially shapeless and it is only by using them that we shape them into ravens or other bird forms, our Breath (Önd) is a flow of energy and hence shapeless, our Hamingja is a basic fluid patch-like form and our Fylgja has shape only due to the fact that its previous possessor gave it characteristics which give rise to its form in the energetic levels of reality, or they adopt archetypal forms from archetypes known by the human collective and match their energetic pattern. This is why so many practices involve shaping various parts of the Self, giving them cohesion which they need to become tools of perception and then able to host our conscious awareness.

Our minds perceive a four-dimensional reality here, these four dimensions being: mass, energy, time and space (or shape, form…). We can only do so through experiences gained in the physical body (Lik). Perception of these four dimensions is the first step to learning to use and manipulate them, which is exactly what is needed for actual High Galdr!

Later on, when we look at expanding the Spark of Self, we will see how our basic skills and understandings of shape enable us to create new forms, which then enable us to interact with other levels of reality. Why need other forms at all? Because the rules of creation dictate that only by taking a shape and hence form – like those beings you wish to communicate with, or which match the dominant one in another level of reality (or even world, if you are thinking in terms of the Nine Worlds) – can you interact with those beings and live in those words. This is a very important skill set which Oðin hints at in stanza 107 of the *Hávamál*:

> "Of a well-assumed form
> I made good use;
> Few things fail the wise;"[29]

For the time being, the importance is in learning about the shape of your physical body (Lik), how it feels to be within it, to perceive from within it, to move it and so forth. We will look at how you can learn the same process belonging to another form when dealing with the Fylgja.

Body Shapes as Energy Indicators

Many people love the saying of you having to look inside for your Self. In fact, this is totally wrong. The inner reflects the outer and the outer in turn reflects the inner. Our physical bodies (Lik) are the central core of our energy body (Hamr) which in turn is a central point of our Spirits (Óðr). When you are looking at someone's physical body (Lik), you are looking at one of the innermost parts of them.

The physical shapes we have are a direct reflection of the state of our health and our energy types as well as energy flows. They are also excellent indicators of how structured the energy body (Hamr) and shadows (Sal) are. Inversely speaking, the stronger the energy body (Hamr) and shadow self (Sal), the better it will result in changes to the physical body (Lik)'s shape.

General rules: the more curvature in your shape, the more complex your energy structures and the greater their scope (diversity). For instance, if you look at muscular man, you will see a massive amount of curvature, where each muscle is shaped in its own distinct way, each one having a curving of physical shape. Compare that to someone who is super slim: this man would have only the most basic shapes making up his limbs and body, while everything else is pretty much straight in comparison. Such an individual would have very simplistic energy systems with far less diversity in energy type than the former.

Fat stored in the body has the energetic effect of slowing it down and making it more sluggish. It is the same with substances such as oils, but there are no slippery effects, energetically speaking. The more fat you carry, the slower your overall vibration will be and the less likely will your energy be to merge with other energy. To be able to be transmitted, the more sluggish and slow its transmission, the less brilliance it will have. Remember, fat cells store surplus energy, toxins and things such as excess stress hormones. Reducing it does not only involve reducing your amount of food intake but also limiting exposure to chemicals, toxins and stress.

Muscle produces energy – both physical and pure energy – in great quantities, and it also speeds up the overall vibrational rates of energy as well as adding to the overall energetic gravity. Too much muscle will slow

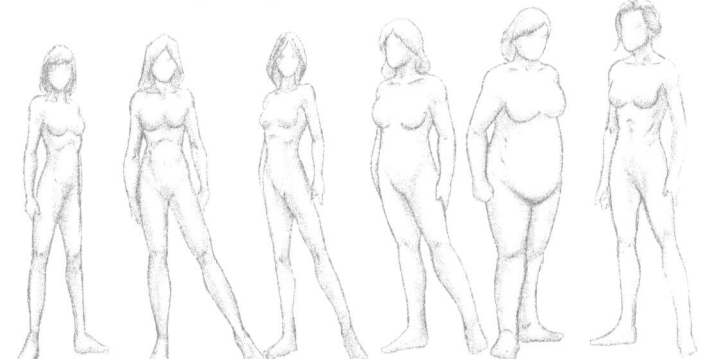

Female body shapes: Slim, Fit, very Slim, Curvy, Fat & Athletic

it down due to the vast increase in energetic gravity. Developing muscle is essential not only to overall health but also to the body's energy system, efficiency and quality.

Brighter skin, hair, nipple and eye tones emit and transfer energy, while darker tones absorb it. The extra melatonin causes this absorption in terms of physical light or energy such as sunlight. Those with thinner hair have highly vibrating spiritual energy. It is more ethereal,

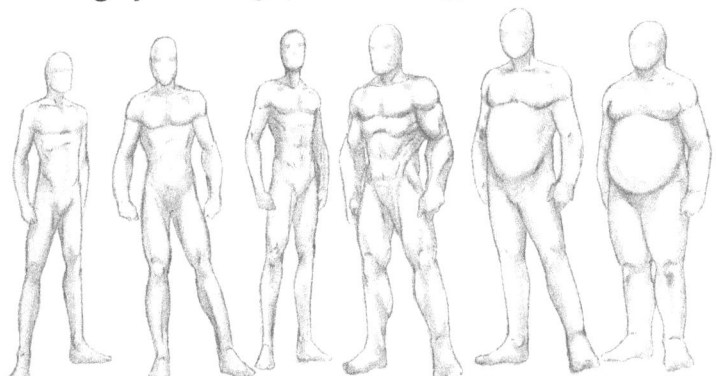

Male body shapes: Slim, Athletic (Swimmer build), very Slim, Atheltic (bodybuilder build), Fat, Obese

whereas those with thicker hair have a stable vibration of energy and are spiritually more grounded – think more earthen. Hence those individuals with the former will have a propensity towards more abstract energy types, whereas those with the latter will be more in tune with nature, elemental and those types of spiritual energies in their environments.

All that is said for the energy in the above descriptions also applies to the energy in general as you have it flowing through you. For instance, if you are a muscular man and you use a runic vocalisation, it will flow much faster and have a much higher vibration than a man who is slim or fat. If you are very muscular, such as a bodybuilder, you will unleash a greater density of energy through your bodies (it will have more punch and greater concentration) but will vibrate at a lower level than would for a man with a muscular swimmer's build. That man would have a higher vibration but less density in his energy flow. Simple. An overweight man would have a very sluggish, low-vibration energy flow, which would move as if it was making its way through sludge and so forth. When men have energy flow, theirs is more fiery and dynamic, while women's is subtler, persistent and more 'together', with longer-term effects in comparison to men's 'more punch and power but only now' patterns.

Impact of Body Form – The Three Fundamental Forces

Having gained a solid understanding of form and its impact, it is time to have a look at how underlying forces give rise to specific forms in manifestation with respect to the human body. This influence comes from what we call the fundamental forces, which manifest our physiology. Each one of us has a specific foundational shape in our bodies. This shape is determined by our genetics, our Spirit (Óðr) and most importantly, our Spark of Self. It cannot be changed even when we adapt or push it towards another shape. No matter how much you want it to change, it will remain fundamentally set. You can make slight changes – you can, by violating the sanctity of the body, make substantial ones at that – but you cannot change the whole of the underlying shape itself. The more fit you are, the less fat you hold, the truer the expression of this fundamental force in your physicality will manifest. It is always odd how people persistently want to force change on their bodies rather than work with what they have. Perfecting your shape is the key, not violating it to make it more like another by violating body sanctity.

These three forces are very simple to understand in elemental terms (we will leave their runic expressions for the time being to avoid overcomplicating things):

Flowing Force: Think of this as a combination of air (or wind) and ice. It is cold, extremely mobile, rapid and flowing. It is delicate and all-pervasive, a balancing force which carries you upwards. Unlike the water type of force, this one is dry – think of air with no humidity. Due to its constantly flowing nature the rapid ability to change from state to state is perfectly expressed by it, as well as an irregular nature. Do not confuse this with being chaotic – it has order within itself but when observed its changing pattern means that it is impossible to fixate a definition of characteristics upon it. Simply, as soon as you try and pin its nature down, it will have changed and become something different.

The Solidifying Force: This force shares characteristics of elemental earth and sea. It has a strong sense of gravity within it, a solidity. It has weight, yet is both solid and soft. Because of its heavy gravity it is very steady, and once on a path it is extremely difficult to throw it off that path. However, unlike the flowing force, the solidifying force moves slowly. In terms of moisture, it has a lot, which almost makes it feel oily to the senses and the richness within it is very comforting and protective (think of it in terms of an overabundance of nutrition).

The Burning Force: This force can be thought

of as a mix of earthly and fire elemental forces. It is hot, dry and has incredible intensity. It is a very sharp and acidic force as well as extremely light. Because of this, it manifests a very penetrating approach to all things it makes contact with. With the earthly influences, rich acidic scents can be picked up when coming into contact with them.

Now that we have a basic view of these three forces, we can see how they dictate our physical body (Lik) shapes. Each body has one of these forces which dictates its shaping. Others can be introduced by willed practices, but even if you overload on any of the other two, all you will achieve is throwing yours out of balance, rather than changing the dominant force dictating your physical shape.

People with flowing force bodies have very fine, almost sculpted lines and curvature in their bodies. Their muscles have a very defined look and they tend not to hold onto much bloating, if any at all. Individuals with this force have thinner and lighter frames than their counterparts and are blessed with a high degree of agility. In terms of builds when perfected at the gym, these individuals will end up with what is often referred to as a 'swimmer's build' and no matter how hard they try, they will not be able to achieve the extremely bulky bodybuilder look. Energy in these individuals is overwhelming but also fades rapidly. It is best compared to a gush of wind which carries everything in its path away and is then gone. These individuals have dry skin, and run colder than their counterparts. In dreamwork, these lucky ladies and gents will have lighter sleep and a tendency towards fully functional consciousness during sleep. Their minds are always running at hyper-speed, thoughts stream faster than others and they often either end up speaking rapidly,

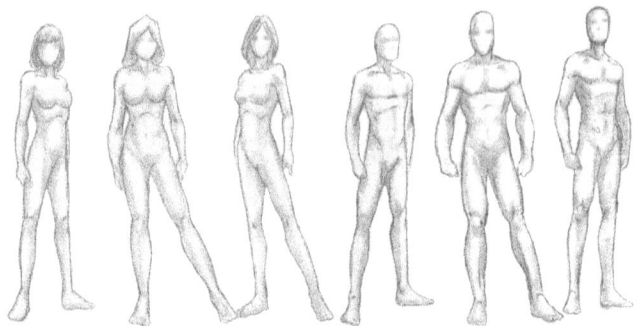

Flow Force body shapes:
(Female) Standard flowing, Strong flowing, Weak flowing,
(Male) Standard flowing, Strong flowing and Weak flowing.

or making incredible jumps in logic which makes it difficult for non-flowing types to follow. They are always on the lookout for new exciting challenges and hate being 'pinned down', even though it would do them a lot of good to be, from time to time.

Those with the solidifying force are practically the opposites of the flowing force individuals. These people have strong builds and a steady flow of constant physical energy. Their frames are larger and they can carry bulk much easier than their counterparts. They have soft and smooth skin (thanks to the moisture in their physio-

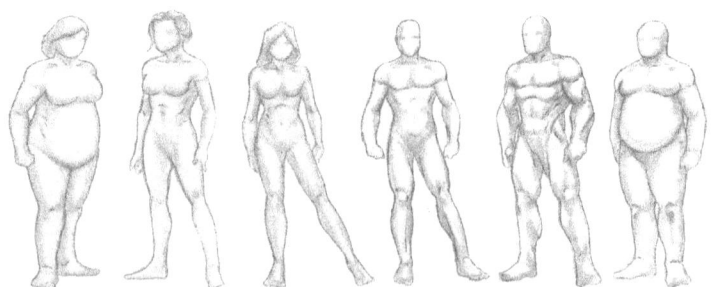

Solidifying Force body shapes:
(Female) Overweight solidifying, Strong solidifying, Standard solidifying
(Male) Standard solidifying, Strong solidifying and Overweight solidifying.

logical force) and very rich, thick hair. It is incredibly easy for them to put weight on. Their minds are far more settled and steadier than those of other types. These individuals have exchanged the ability to reach the heights of those of the flowing force, for the ability to maintain stability effortlessly. In effect, unlike the flowing force individuals, the solidifying ones will not rapidly shift from ecstasy to depression in a cyclic manner, but will maintain an overall balanced midpoint between those two extremes.

Individuals who are of the burning force body type are typically medium sized in body frame. They have excellent digestive systems, seem to have an endless

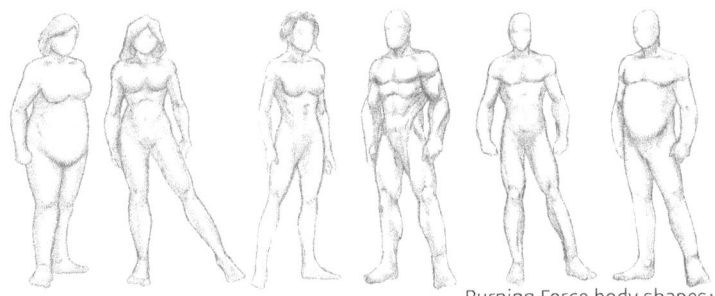

Burning Force body shapes:
(Female) Overweight burning, Athletic burning, Standard burning,
(Male) Athletic burning, Standard burning and Overweight burning

store of energy, high sex drives and can be very predisposed to hair loss. Their bodies are always warm and they adapt very rapidly to both hot and cold climates. Putting weight on is easy for these lucky ones but they have difficulty handling that additional weight. These individuals have a tendency to be either in great shape or fat – it is the one or the other. Their minds are very rapid in comparison to the solidifying individuals, but somewhat slower than the flowing ones. The burning force individuals are very direct and outspoken. They will tell you exactly what they think, whether you like it or not, unlike the reserved flowing force minds. These men and women are a hive of activity in their own right: constant challenges, constant new ventures, the more the better!

These basic forces, one of which gave rise to your shape, will dictate ALL the tendencies and manifestations of the Self. Remember, your physical body (Lik) shape dictates the shapes of practically all other parts of the Self. They will also dictate how your runic energies manifest. For instance, a ᚠ Fé (Fehu) fire rune for the burning types will be the most explosive energy you can get, the same rune for the flowing types will be the furthest reaching and quickest expansive manifestation of the fires and for the solidifying types, it will be the hottest and most tangible. They also dictate how strong one's work is on each of the three levels of reality, where the solidifying types will have the greatest advantages on the energetic levels (Lik, Hamr and Sal), the burning types will have the main advantage at the mental level (Óðr, Hugr, and Minni) and the flowing types on the archetypal (Önd, Hamingja and Fylgja). Needless to say, most "advantage" does not mean the other types cannot function on those levels – it will just be a little more of a challenge for them, that is all. We will be returning to these three forces at many other points in time. It is a good idea to get a basic grasp of them here.

A Few Words on Muscle

Muscle is an endocrine organ. It is also a substantial biological energy generator. Men here have a massive advantage in their ability to add muscular bulk. However, knowing how to use that bulk is key. All too often, these days we often see people in a state of being fat, overweight or so slim that they look like a skeleton wrapped in skin with a thin layer of flesh. Both these states are highly unhealthy, irrespective of what the mainstream and health movements are trying to promote. Let us look at the underlying reasons as to why this is the case (in energetic terms).

Human muscle is used by our bodies to produce force and motion by using energy. It is also an endocrine organ which controls the balance of catabolic and anabolic functions in the body. From an energetic point of view, muscle is essential for two key reasons: it produces energy and condenses it, but not only that, it is used to store it as well. When the muscle fibres contract (especially with skeletomuscular) they make the produced energy vibrate as well as releasing the stored energy. It literally causes a vibrational stream or wave to radiate out. The more muscle you have, the more powerful those vibrational waves, the more of them occur and the longer they last. The smooth muscle in our bodies causes the energies to flow with a gentler force along the path of their fibres. This is both a transformational function and a carrier one, where the explosive energies released by the skeletomuscular fibres are softened and made to flow through the soft muscle tissue. Needless to say, having as much muscle as possible will give you the most benefit in terms of energy. In addition, we will see at a later point in time how to use muscle to condense and make semi-physical runic energy. The average adult male has about 6% more muscle mass than the average adult woman[30] and due to their ability to build muscle, men can greatly increase their muscle mass, which they should do as a matter of utmost importance. **It is the MOST significant spiritual development step anyone can take.**

The main reason for us being in bodies of flesh and those forming the apex of the energetic level of the Self indicates just how important the physical body (Lik) actually is to our entire being. Most will think that cannot be right, surely? How can the body have such a profound impact and function? Unfortunately for everyone, it is, and it is a reality which is deeply mystical in its own right. We will go into this below. Since the mind (Hugr) and the energy body (Hamr) are not naturally directly connected, we struggle in reaching it and its perceptive mechanisms. More often than not, reaching the energy body (Hamr) requires substantial energy reserves which are free (not used by other physiological or mental processes). As discussed in *The Spirit of Húnir Awakens – Parts 1 & 2* there is very scarce if any of this free energy in mankind, so amplifying the physiological sources and stores of energy is an essential step in increasing our total available energy.

A Few Words on The Nervous System

The nervous system is the main communication network for our physical body (Lik) and its energy systems. Very large portions of the scientific community are trying to study and learn as much about it as possible. There is much information and disinformation out there about its capabilities and functions. For our purpose, we will leave those specifics for another discussion and instead take a brief look at the energetic side of things. The spine and the nervous system flowing out of it are the anchor of your Self. They are also what one grounds into. When people talk about having to ground and all that nonsense, what they fail to realise is that the very fact that we are in physical bodies means we ARE grounded. If you need to reaffirm your foothold, all you do is focus on your spine, feel it and pull your energy into it. It is easy to do because that is the energetic function of the spine – just will or intend it and it will work. Energy flows through the nervous system – both physical energy and non-physical. Before engaging in too much energy and runic work, it is an excellent idea to find a proper chiropractor and make sure the spine is properly functioning and loosened with an adjustment or two. The difference it makes is very acute when trying to make energy flow through it.

We will look at the spine and brain in a lot of detail at a later point in time. For the time being, it is worth keeping in mind that the nervous system is the communication network of your biological awareness. In other words, it is even more important than you could have suspected.

 # Sanctity of the Body

We have seen how important an impact the physical body (Lik) has on not only our energy body (Hamr) and our shadow self (Sal) but also how it interacts or rather allows our Spirit (Óðr) to interact with the world around us. Our minds (Hugur), memory (Minni) and Spirits (Óðr) need a fully functional body in order to fully express themselves. The biological awareness, merged with our conscious awareness, is the key to our evolution and can only be fully mastered within our physical bodies (Lik). Finally, achieving the full union of the Self and triggering the Spark of Self expansion makes biological awareness essential. When we violate the body, be it via deliberate intoxication, pointless medical procedures, unnecessary suffering of its internal organisms and so forth, we are turning that awareness against our own conscious minds and disrupting its relationship with our Self.

This is the main reason why it is important for us to not only nurture and protect our bodies and develop a good solid pattern of communications with our biological awareness, but also to actively look out for any potential actions which might disrupt all this. This is what in the old days was meant when we referred to the 'sanctity of the body' being paramount. Even when having to undergo medical procedures which are life and death ones, they will need to be undertaken with great care and we must develop our biology's understanding that this is the case before doing so. We must always, under all circumstances, respect our bodies and avoid putting them under undue risk or danger. We should avoid 'breaking it', harming it, introducing harmful things into it or sharing it (or parts of it) out 'willy-nilly' with everyone. Yes, that means the rune mystic avoids at all costs giving blood, donating organs and so forth (or accepting them from another, for that matter). All these weaken the Self or introduce another's Self into your own. Both are essentially disruptions of the Self in one shape or another. Let us take a closer look at the medical side of things.

Body and Medication

Where to start? This is a complex and controversial topic to deal with but something does need to be said about it. We as a species are being drowned in medication, be it medically prescribed or self-administered. It is not an issue of drugs, it is an issue of lifestyle and conditioned belief that as soon as something is wrong, as soon as the body tells us via pain or discomfort that something is amiss, we rush for a pill or some form of medicine to fix it.

Now the views on medication can range from one extreme to the other. We are either faced with the argument that it is all good and needed for some reason or another and that without it, life is impeded or limited or even impossible in some fashion or other, or at the other extreme, any form of medication is seen as unnecessary or wrong in some way or other. Neither of these is advisable – there is a reason why medication and chemicals of these types exist and our approach should be one of balance and understanding. Sometimes they are needed, but most of the time they are not and in some cases they cause more harm than good, whilst in others, they can be very helpful.

Let us look at types of medications:

Those which block, take away or change some physiological responses – from the energy point of view and the phisical body (Lik) itself (its biological awareness). These types of medications are the most harmful. It is the equivalent of the limited human mind and limited sciences saying 'We know better than your vast biological intelligence which has evolved for millennia'. What is worse, it literally forcefully overrides the body's natural processes. These types of medications, drugs or processes cause the most disharmony and conflict with the underlying body's physiological intelligence and are the hardest to repair. It is on par with what has been said about short-circuiting the will with respect to hypnosis in *The Spirit of Húnir Awakens*.

Those which add to the physiological responses – these ones are a bit more hit and miss than the former. If you are adding something which the biology perceives as beneficial to it, you will increase its harmony with you. If you are adding something it dislikes or disapproves of, or is a hindrance for it to deal with, you will face the same issues as with the medication types outlined above. Remember, our biology is trying to complete its own evolution and anything which inhibits it or takes too much energy away from it is seen as harmful. When looking at this issue, it is hard for us because we often see the body as ours, as a tool or a part of us, and we seldom consider the fact that it is indeed a separate universe of life forms which we need to look after and help evolve.

Those which replace or enable a lacking or defective physiological response – these types of medications are often seen as highly beneficial and immensely increase the harmony with the biological intelligence. Under this category are all the things used to restore optimal functions such as probiotics, vitamins, minerals, inhalers for asthmatics, insulin for diabetics, probiotics for digestion and so forth.

Those which enhance physiological processes – these are a bit tricky as well. Typically, the biology will react in a negative manner and as time passes, it shifts into a highly positive one. It just takes a little time for it to 'observe' what is happening and to experience it. It is important to keep one key thing in mind: whatever processes or functions are enhanced, it must not be at the expense of the biology itself. Should that occur, it will see it as a threat. This is why nano-technology will always impact it in a highly negative fashion. The biology simply sees this as something alien trying to attack and take away from it – which technically speaking, it is. Nano-bots which take over the biological processes are a direct violation of the integrity of the biological awareness and the sanctity of the body. Thankfully, we are yet to get to that point.

Surgeries – where to start on this one. They should be avoided at all costs if possible. In some cases, they are life-saving and totally necessary, but in all other cases they should be avoided. These days, when cosmetic surgery has become so popular, we often forget that the body shapes itself the way it is with the characteristics and features it has for a very specific reasons. Forcefully, by violence against it, changing it will more often than not cause permanent disruptions in the harmony of the physical body (Lik). Sometimes this can be so severe that it will spill over into other parts of the Self. The best case scenario is that the physical body (Lik) will lock you out of biological awareness completely. The worst – well, who wants to contemplate that? In most cases, the more severe the surgery, the greater the resulting friction with, in some cases, the physical body (Lik) throwing out the Spirit (Óðr) completely.

The vitally important thing to keep in mind is that we need the biological awareness to grow with us, or our unification of the Self will fail. Additionally, the physical body (Lik) is the key to both the energy body (Hamr) and the shadow (Sal), which means the actual energetic skills, perceptions and mastery are hindered by a negative relationship with our bodies.

MYSTERIES OF BLOOD AND DNA

Blood - Crystallised Megin and Life Essence

Since the dawn of time, blood has been held as sacred and the substance which gives life by mankind. It has given rise to countless traditions, rituals, medical processes, and to fiction, and has been the trigger of creative and destructive events throughout human history.

In our modern area, we know the medical and biological functions of blood all too well and we keep discovering more. Blood has not only become a taboo subject but something to be feared, mostly due to the transmission of all-too-often debilitating life-long diseases. However, blood is still well known for being an essential key criterion for life. For our purposes, we are going to look a little deeper than just the medical side of blood, for much has been forgotten and some of those forgotten characteristics of blood are essential in our work.

Blood and The Physical Body (Lik)

As far as anatomy is concerned, blood is a special type of connective tissue originating in the bones. It is highly adaptive in terms of being a carrier both for physiological functions and energetic ones. Its ability to carry light is clear from its change in colour, where arterial blood is lighter and redder than venous blood (which is very dark red), as a result of the amount of oxygen in it.[31] Do take note of this light carrier function of blood – it will be of importance in our discussions.

The main functions of blood in our body (Lik) can be summarised as it being a carrier of the 'signals' and 'elements' needed for life. It supplies oxygen and nutrients to tissues, removes waste, circulates white blood cells (hence has immunity functions), regulates body temperature, has hydraulic functions, acts as a messenger transporting hormones, nutrients (and much more) between tissues and organs and has repair functions where it can shift from liquid into a semi-solid gel-like form when it coagulates to seal wounds.

Due to its liquid nature, it has the ability to carry energy of all types. In terms of physiology, this is will mainly be the electric and magnetic currents of energy flowing throughout the energy system but it is by no means limited to those by any stretch of the imagination.

The blood is composed of three cell 'structures' (for want of a better term). You have the red blood cells, the white blood cells and the platelets. This connects our very blood to the principles of trinity. We have the red cells which are manifestations of Muspelheim, the white cells connected to Niflheim and the platelets which are connected to Midgard. The red cells carry oxygen, nutrients and so forth. They have a direct role in energy production they are the carrier of life and fire themselves. The white blood cells, on the other hand, are produced by our immune systems in order to combat infections, viruses and other foreign bodies. This enables the body to maintain a healthy status quo. The connection to Niflheim is very straightforward. It is the world of stasis which is yet another form of maintenance of the 'status quo' (homeostasis). Additionally, as we have seen, Niflheim holds the initial waters (ice melted by heat from Muspelheim) which gave rise to life – after all, water is a product of the mix of ice and fire. We will look at the specifics of the nature of water elsewhere. For now, it is important to keep in mind that it is the universal carrier containing both primal forces and influences (those of ice and fire). The blood is so similar to water that its average density is close to that of pure water. They are practically identical (the average density of blood is 1060 kg/m3 while the density of pure water is 1000 kg/m3).[32] Another fascinating point to consider is that the total amount of blood in our bodies is 7% of our body weight.[33-34] You might wonder why this number is of any concern. It is simply due to the fact that seven is the number of the rune X Gjöf (Gebo), which is the rune of exchange. This fits very well with the function of blood as a transporter and carrier mechanism.

Finally, we have the third point of this trinity in blood: the platelets. It is interesting to see that when they are involved, we have a radical shift from pure liquid into a thick gel-like and finally hard substance. This is a typical condensation and increase in matter (rather than energy) which occurs in Midgard. The importance of blood cannot be overstated. It is all pervasive in our bodies and floods practically each and every part of our physiology.

Energetic Nature of Blood

The important key to consider when looking at the energetic side of blood is that it carries not only physical energy but also pure energy, which in turn feeds the energy body (Hamr) and the Shadow self (Sal). Naturally, the distribution is primarily skewed towards physical energy – that is its nature by default. Because of its carrier functionality (both in biological and energetic terms), we can increase the amount of non-physical energy flowing through it. Before we take the leap into this, you should keep in mind, as mentioned above, that blood is a crystallisation (or condensation, if you prefer) of Megin and life force. This is the reason why it nourishes our organs and tissues. It is due to the life force – or to be more precise, life essence (these are transported within the red blood cells) and the reason for growth and regeneration is the Megin.

Here is a secret of blood for you to consider. It gives energy cohesion (that is the energetic function of white blood cells), and the platelet energetic function is to condense it and finally, the red blood cells, due to their circular non-flat shape, can contain and transport this energy in the flow of blood. These energetic functions of various blood cells are what makes it so vitally important in energy work of all kind. It is also why in ancient times our ancestors used to 'bleed' the runes. This refers to writing them out in blood. This did not only cause the runic energies to be condensed, given cohesion (so that they can be used with intent) and structured into form or given shape (allowing them to manifest in the energetic level of reality), but additionally, because blood is in effect a water fluid (with a few additional extras), it acts as a cross-reality transport mechanism, allowing energy to be bridged from one level of reality into another. Now that you have knowledge of all these functions of blood, it is easy to logic out the reason for preferring blood to any other form of ink. It allows the blood to act as a gateway or connection device in between the pure energy levels of reality and the physical. Then this runic energy is condensed into shape (the shape of the rune), and given cohesion, allowing it to be manipulated without it naturally dissipating and to be activated by sound (when you vocalise the rune's name).

Blood and 'Personalised' Life Force

'Blood is life' has long been a common saying amongst mankind. This is due to the fact that life force flows through blood and vitalises every organ and tissue in our bodies, as well as providing life essence for our energy body (Hamr). This is not just generic life force, and for this reason, when so-called 'healers' try to heal the physical body (Lik) with either their own or universal life force, it never 'sticks'. This is due to the fact that our bodies need what you can think of as personalised life force, which is specifically attuned to your body with your essences. Think of life force as an energy which is the product of a specific combination of all the elemental and runic forces. For instance, let us say that your life force contains all runic energies but has a spread of stronger ᚠ Fé (Fehu) (say 110%), weaker ᛁ Íss (Isa) (80%), double the amount of ᚲ Kaun (Kenaz) (200%) and ᚦ Þurs (Thurisaz) (200%), whereas the other rune energies are at their normal intensity (100%). This is just a generic example but this sort of energetic spread occurs in each of us. In the above example, in order to get a compatible life force, you would have to use 100% of each rune, except a 110% of ᚠ Fé (Fehu), only an 80% of ᛁ Íss (Isa) and a double amount of both ᚲ Kaun (Kenaz) and ᚦ Þurs (Thurisaz). Combining all these in the correct amounts and producing a single harmonised essence to heal a patient with that life force would mean you get effective healing. This should give you a general idea of what is meant by a personalised life force.

This is also why certain people get on well together, whilst others cannot stand the sight of each other and seem to only need the smallest trigger to turn on one another. It all boils down to the interaction of runic energies – or to be more precise, the balance of those energies in each persons' life essence. Fascinating occurrences can take place, especially with two individuals who have complimentary dynamics of rune energies in their life essence. This is also the root of our attraction and ease of interaction with certain runes and difficulty with others. For instance, in our example above, that individual would find it incredibly easy to work with the ᚲ Kaun (Kenaz) and ᚦ Þurs (Thurisaz) runes but would really struggle with the ᛁ Íss (Isa) one. Our blood contains this personalised life force, whereas our DNA contains the encodings for it – in other words, the instructions on which runes and what amount of those runic energies and what vibrational frequency of each rune's energy need to be combined in order to generate this personalised life force.

It is important to keep two things in mind when dealing with this. Each individual has a totally unique 'mix' of energies which make up his or her life essence. In addition to this, we are not only dealing with energy but also information. All of our life experiences end up encoded as frequencies of life essence, and the product of them is what we call life essence (personal life force + personal and ancestral life experiences). This is what, in the most basic manifestation, produces blood types and is also one of the main reasons why you cannot receive blood from anyone but only specific people, or you risk death. Biologically, it is an issue of chemistry. Energetically, it is an issue of conflicting types of energies in the life essence trying to overcome each other, resulting in a breakdown of both.

Because of this, the blood carries the Self within it and is why the Spirit (Óðr) can blend with it. This is one of the main reasons why blood is often considered 'sacred'. For our purposes, a runic mystic should at all costs avoid taking another's blood, as it would introduce a lesser well-developed blood with its life essence into his or her own Self. Using the runic energies, the blood of the rune mystic is purified and its vibrational level is increased beyond what it was. It then makes it less and less compatible with typical human blood types. By the same logic, rune mystics never ever donate blood because they know that their blood will disrupt anyone it is given to. The runic energy concentration within it quickly overpowers lesser concentrations and frequencies, disrupting the balance and threatening the very stability of the life essence of any potential recipient.

For those of you interested in energetic mathematics, you will see that we are, in effect, in possession of a triple trinity within our very blood. The initial is the physical: red cells, white cells and platelets connecting us to the fires (Muspelheim), the ice (Niflheim) and the earth (Midgard). The second trinity is found in the energetic characteristics: it carries life force, life essence and Megin. The final trinity is in the functionality of blood: cohesion, condensation and shaping. This triple trinity is the basis of the Self in the physical.

Blood in The Traditional Context

Blood in Germanic traditions was used during the Blóts (these were mainly forms of ritualistic sacrifices for worship). They would occur at prescribed times of the year, after successful battles and so forth, and they could involve sacrifices to the Gods, Goddesses, spirits, ancestors, Elves and so forth. An additionally interesting hint is that the Blóts were also used to 'strengthen'.[35] In this context, blood was seen as possessing the power of its originator and would be used to soak the status, participants and temples in power.

Blood is also mentioned in countless other traditions, ranging from the more ancient ones to the modern ones where Christianity makes mention of the 'blood of Christ' in its rituals.

An interesting usage of blood is also found in indigenous Australians, where a mixture of red ochre and blood is used in rituals where participants cover themselves in it. In the secret male ceremonies, venous blood is extracted from participants and rubbed over each other's bodies. These ceremonies of sacred masculine 'brotherhood' are highly secret, so details of their purposes and nature are very seldom available for us to inspect. However, by looking at the symbiosis produced by blood and energy, we can make certain logical deductions. We have seen how blood carries the power and properties of the Self and is connected to the Breath of Oðin as it flows through our energetic and physical selves. Exchanging blood with a male gives you access to his creative power as well. These ceremonies make a strong bond between the participants, creating a tribal creative and highly life-giving collective, sharing strength and power throughout all members. They also enhance the flow of (personalised) life force and balance it out throughout all members. For instance, should one of these men be more specialised in certain forms of life force expression, it will manifest within him and then spread to all the others, making accessible to them something which they would otherwise not have. In exchange, their own specialisations are made to that male. It literally allows each member to grow and be exposed to new life force, powers and characteristics which he would not be able to on his own.

Blood and the Runes

Naturally runes and blood are deeply intertwined. We have seen above how the rune masters of old used their own blood to 'bleed the runes' but now it is time for a deeper look at this and more specifically how to make practical use of it.

One important thing to keep in mind is that our blood carries within it far more than just life force and power or energetic signature. It carries our DNA and that in itself establishes a powerful linkage to the runes as human DNA through the chromosomes. We will look at this in more detail elsewhere, but the human genome contains two copies of 23 chromosomes, the first 22 present in every person are directly related to the initial 22 runes. The 23rd ᛞ Dagur (Dagaz) rune is found in the X sex chromosome, and finally the male-only Y chromosome serves as an anchor point for the ᛟ Óðal (Othala) rune.

By making the runes synchronise with the relevant chromosomes and by flooding the blood with Megin, we awaken the power of the rune and its rune stream in our very blood, empowering it and hence ourselves. The rune mystic who achieves this embodiment of ALL runes (in the case of men, all 24, in women, the first 23) in their blood achieves the embodiment of creation within themselves. They are then able to bleed the runes by spilling their own blood into the shape of the runes whilst enlivening them with High Galdr. In this fashion, we unlock the potential power dormant in our blood and in the runes. It is very much like using the blood as a carrier for the rune stream.

Embodiment of Runic Energy Into The Blood

This is going to be the only practice to do with blood (at this point in time). There is only one because it is both a foundational practice and an enabling one. What it does is simply allow you to achieve what was discussed above. This takes time but produces very distinctive and observable results (to those who care for such observations). Each rune has a specific effect on your blood and you should never overuse individual runes. They all serve to balance each other out and as such, skipping even one can produce adverse effects which would then need to be corrected before you were able to move on with your work. The only choice you have is splitting the runes into the traditional sets known as Ætts and working with them each, rather than having to do all the runes at one time (which can be quite a challenge, and it is an even greater one to keep it up!). Hence we are going to focus on the Ætt which are three sets of eight runes each.

The first eight runes will awaken the 'potentials' in your blood, the ancestral (inherited) gifts and personal Spark of Self characteristics, which are dormant within and activate them all.

The second eight runes will enhance the powers within your blood. They increase the energetic gravity, they enhance the expression of force and Megin within it, and amplify energetic condensation. Many will be tempted to just use the runes of this Ætt but doing so exclusively will put a massive strain on your system (both energetic and physical). It is always best to do the second Ætt before the third and after the first! There is a reason why it is the second! The first will prepare your bodies for the second, which in turn will prepare your Self for the effects of the third.

The third Ætt brings expansion of Self, a type of stretching of the influences from the physical (dense energetic), through the energetic, the mental and the archetypal. They stretch the conscious awareness into the other parts of the Self and make it easier to crossover various parts of the Self in preparation for unity within the Self.

It is important to remember that these functions of the Ætts are ONLY in relation to their use within the blood! When using them on other parts of our physiology, different effects are obtained. Please avoid stretching these definitions to areas they do not belong in.

The actual practice is built on those found in 'Awakening the Breath of Oðin'.[36] The important thing is to allow your Megin to flow through your body. As soon as you feel it flowing, you are ready to move into this practice. Each time you do it, ensure you have a clear sensation of the Megin's flow. Keep it in focus during the entire practice. Because you have been keeping focus on your blood flow, you will have also spread your awareness into it. The next step involves a simple reflection on the fact that you are flowing through your blood. This shift in perspective will anchor you in the actual blood rather than you just observing and feeling it as a third party – you will be flowing within it, you ARE the blood flowing through your body. It is a simple shift in perspective and nothing more – there are no steps here, so just keep in mind that you are the blood, and the shift will occur. It is that simple because, in fact, you ARE the blood! It is an intrinsic part of your Self. This is why you do not need any steps or stages or transfers of conscious awareness or anything else.

Once you are comfortable with being the blood and flowing through your physical body (Lik), feel the energy, the Megin, and the energetic gravity flowing through the blood – through you! It is a sensation, a type of pulse, an almost tangible strength to watch out for. If you are having trouble picking it up, simply intend yourself to do so. Intent is both the key and the lock in this type of work. The final part of this practice is to vocalise the rune out loud whilst keeping the focus of you being the blood. It is quite a simple one to do, and the 'trick' involves vocalising the rune but not paying attention to doing so. Rather, pay attention to the vibration of the rune's name or sound coming from the blood itself (remember, you are the blood at this point!). As it does, it will flood you (the blood) and you will feel its energy flow.

In this practice, always keep the runic energy colour to a deep red. This should not be difficult since it is the traditional colour used to visualise and draw the runes in the first place. As for sensations, they are not necessary. They only become so when you start using

High Galdr instead of simply vocalising the runes. If you are doing so, you will have access to the information on each rune's characteristics and there is no need to repeat them here.

When done, refocus on your physical body (Lik), let the awareness of your blood – of being your blood – fade away and be replaced by your typical awareness of your physical body (Lik). Take a breath or two and open your eyes.

Never ever vocalise the rune more than three times in your blood. There is absolutely no point overloading it. Remember, any overworking here will not only effect your blood but will also spill into every organ and every cell of your entire body, every filament of your energy body and every pulse of your shadow body (Sal). Please take it slow, one step at a time, one rune at a time. We want to grow, not harm ourselves because of some stupid concept of having to rush through things. It is self-destructive to rush these things.

Quick Steps

1 Ensure you have a good sense of the flow of Megin in your blood. Keep focus on it during the entire practice.

2 Spend a few minutes in reflection on the fact that you are your blood. It carries your very essence within it – your personalised life force, if you prefer, to each and every organ within your body.

3 Keep on focussing that you are the blood until your perceptions shift to include only the sense of blood and you flowing within it.

Bring back into your awareness the sensation of the Megin flowing within it. Once you have a firm awareness of this, you are ready for runic work.

4   Keeping your focus on the fact that you are your blood, vocalise out loud the rune you wish to work with. It is best to keep all runic energy visualised as deep red in this practice (making it highly compatible with your blood). The main trick here is to feel it being vocalised by your very blood. Remember, that is your focal point not your head (well, for this practice in any case)! It is the blood which is calling out the rune's energy, it is in the blood that it manifests and it is the blood which it affects. Simple, highly effective and to the point.

5   As you vocalise the rune's name, see and feel its energy flooding the entire bloodstream and merging with it. Remember to only do this a maximum of three times for each rune (providing you are not overly sensitive to that rune! If you are, once will do).

For clarity's sake, you should start with the first Ætt runes as given in their traditional order: ᚠ Fé (Fehu), ᚢ Úr (Uruz), ᚦ Þurs (Thurisaz), ᚨ Óss (Ás) (Ansuz), ᚱ Reið (Raidho), ᚲ Kaun (Kenaz), ᚷ Gjöf (Gebo) and finally ᚹ Vin (Wunjo). Only use each one once to begin with until you have completed the row. Then take a break for a few days. When you come back to the practice, repeat the same but increase it to two vocalisations per rune before moving onto the next one, and so forth, until you complete the row with three vocalisations for each rune. At that point, you can tackle the following eight runes. Do not skip runes and stick to the Ætt (rune sets of eight) in their natural order. See Appendix A for more information on the runes. Those listed from 1 to 8 (inclusive) are your first Ætt runes, those running from 9 to 16 (inclusive) are your second and 17 to 24 are your final set.

    A few effects to keep in mind are: arousal for the runes which have strong sexual currents, a boost in energy for those which relate to physicality or strength, a rise in blood pressure and heat for the fire-related runes, a cold sensation for their icy counterparts, the feeling of being solid (especially for ᚢ Úr (Uruz) and ᛟ Óðal (Othala)) and the spontaneous awakening of memories (with ᛗ Dagur (Dagaz) and ᛜ Ing (Ingwaz)) as well as emotions (ᛒ Bjarkan (Berkano) and ᛚ Lögur (Laguz)). There are ample others, but these are ones to keep an eye out for. If you are elderly, be careful with the fire runes and the increase in blood pressure. Should it occur, do not increase the number of times you vocalise that specific rune further. Ageing decreases the overall energetic resistance capacity of our bodies and we can only expose it to so much of an energy increase. If you get the spike in heat and blood pressure at a single vocalisation, stay at one and progress with the following rune regardless.

The Blood of Lóðurr Awakens

Human Deoxyribonucleic Acid (DNA)

Human DNA is an important part of us, not only in terms of our physical body (Lik) but also in terms of our energy body (Hamr) and shadow Self (Sal). As we have mentioned time and again, these three parts of the Self exist and function on the energy level of reality, each at a certain level of energy-matter density, but all are nonetheless energy. In addition to this, this is our foundation, and it is from this level that the human spirit rises and births its Self. Our DNA can be thought of as being a product of:

1. Ancestral or inherited DNA
2. Viral and bacterial DNA – any bio-organism which lives in and infects the human being
3. Environmental and chemical DNA
4. Spiritually sourced DNA (from Fylgja, and for firstborn males, the kin-Fylgja)
5. Memories and experiences encoded in DNA
6. And soon, if technology keeps on infecting the human organism, we might have to include data stored in DNA as part of our DNA.

Which are beneficial or not is debatable. In any case, most engineered, viral and potentially the data DNA are hindrances – or if you prefer, corruptions – of our DNA structures. Memories and experiences can also be very harmful. Negative ones introduce loops of energy loss in the DNA structures – or you can think of them as gaps. The introduction of non-living or interfering DNA into any living organism is the equivalent of creating gaps within it. In other words, technology is introducing the essence of the Ginnungagap (the Great Nothing), into the very structures of the building blocks of life.

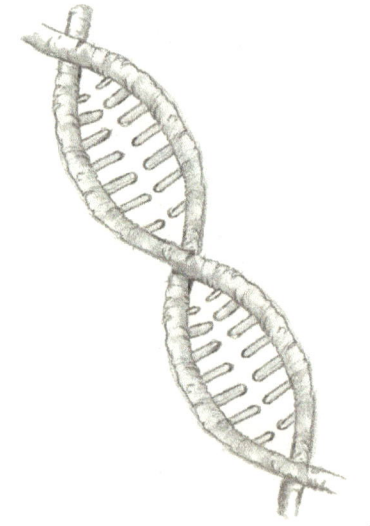

DNA Strand

Some will argue that the DNA listed under no two above is not relevant because it is found in addition to human DNA. For instance, the concept of an invading organism being there, as a separate 'bio-life form' to that of the human being and hence its own DNA, would be its own rather than part and parcel of the human genome. This might be correct in some instances, but not as a general rule. The introduction of any genetic material has the potential to affect our whole genome.

Some viruses in effect target human DNA and write themselves into it.[37-38] This is how the whole process takes place when trying to do genetic editing (which, let us be clear, is a very hit-and-miss science, even these days!).

Rather than have a whole book dedicated to the sciences of DNA, we are going to have a quick look at some of its broad functions and switch immediately to the energetic side of things which is the primary focus of this. The more complex and advanced uses and the function of DNA can be looked at in detail at a later point in time.

Purpose of DNA

To scientists, DNA can be summarised as carrying out a key number of essential functions in the form of genetic instructions: it controls the formation, growth reproduction and functioning of all the building blocks for life. At present, we understand the structure of DNA to be that of a double helix. Each strand is composed of repeating units called nucleotides, and these in turn are made of elements represented by the well known four letters C, G, A and T – representing the four bases for DNA: cytosine, guanine, adenine and thymine – which we are told is the entire code base for life. Incidentally, we have now a fifth and sixth contender which have been 'discovered'.[39-40] Interesting, is it not? How things resolve to a 3, 6 or 9!

The structure of DNA is dynamic along its length, being capable of coiling into tight loops, and other shapes.[41] This coiling can be very tight (and is then termed supercoiled) in a positive direction, where it pulls in the helixes towards each other more tightly, or in a negative direction where it causes them to loosen up and given sufficient loosening, makes them fall apart. This falling apart can also be due to external influencing factors, most notably electro-magnetic radiation such as WiFi, cellphones, IT equipment radiation and so forth. (See Appendix C - Dangers of WiFi to Human Health and DNA.)

    DNA is typically structured as linear or circular forms of chromosomes. In humans, we have 46 chromosomes,[42] inherited from our parents. We get 23 from each parent, but the 23rd differs, where from our mother we get an X chromosome and from our father, boys get the Y chromosome whereas girls get an additional X chromosome. This produces the all-too-famous XY or XX sex-determining chromosome. What is not really well known is that in girls, one of the copies of the X is deactivated (this process is called X-inactivation or lyonization in scientific terminology) meaning they technically have 45 activated chromosomes, rather than 46. This is just a broad estimate, due to the fact that in our genome we have many inactive genes and hence a completely accurate count of active and inactive genes is at this point in time impossible.

    Now, you might be justified in thinking what on earth all this has to do with energy and the runes. A very valid question. Time for us to have a look at those! DNA is not only physical (which, let me remind you, is nothing more or less than the densest form of energy, but energy nonetheless: matter = condensed or compressed energy) but also has many energetic functions. We know that our bodies (yes, the physical ones!) produce light and electromagnetism, and we actually measure those with various clinical and research devices such as EEGs and influence them by others such as

TMS (transcranial magnetic stimulation). Our neutrons produce electric impulses which shift to chemical (neurotransmitters), then back to electric. The heart and our brains produce both electric and magnetic fields and so on. In addition to all these energetic characteristics of our physiology, our DNA produces light and electric currents. This is a field into which science is currently trying to make big strides as it attempts to add light switches into the genome and then, by using radio-waves, turning those on and off, thereby enabling and disabling gene expression. Both are potentially wonderful and utterly horrific in scope of application,[43-44] as many have for a long time been thought safe and have now been discovered to produce quite significant side-effects, such as the "unintended long-term change in brain function", impairing cognitive functioning, causing seizures[45] and even psychotic symptoms (delusions).[46] You can find more about this entire field, should you be interested, by looking for 'optogenetic switch' in scientific publications.

With this approach, what we see is a bridging of the modern day sciences with the old runic insights provided by our ancestors. We not only have the light/electricity linkage but also further insights into how the biological genome is interlinked with the energy body (Hamr) and shadow (Sal), as well as the physical body (Lik)'s energy systems. Let us take a quick look at the chromosomes: there are 22 of them, in addition to the X sex chromosome and the Y sex chromosome, totalling a set of 24 individual chromosome combinations in the human genome (remember, the 23rd is a mix of two Xs or one X and a Y). Lights flashing yet? What if you were told that each of these is directly linked to one of the 24 runes? Ah, the 'ah ha' moment hits! This is why in all our practices and discussions, when we look at the pure feminine, we exclude the ᚩ Óðal (Othala) rune. That rune is anchored in the Y chromosome which is not present in women's genome. Avoid going into the train of thought that this is: 1) a bad thing, and 2) an inferior state of being – neither are correct as we will see shortly. It is the rune which physiologically speaking gives men larger bodies, more strength and so forth. It also links them more firmly with their physicality. It is also the reason why women have a more fluid and adaptable energy type. The lack of the ᚩ Óðal (Othala) rune to bind things down, to define and solidify, is what gives women that enormous advantage when it comes to energy work. Men have their 'castle', represented by ᚩ Óðal (Othala), which is their body. Women do not and are free to explore due to their increased fluidity (and flexibility). This gives them the ability to anchor themselves beyond the purely physical (and might explain why they more readily manifest increased intuition and pre-cognitive perceptions). Each gender has a plus and a minus when it comes to the ᚩ Óðal (Othala) influence or the lack thereof, and that is a discussion for another time and place (when looking at polarities). For the time being, the important point to keep in mind is that each of these chromosomes is a direct expression of runic influences and energies in the human Being. The other anchor for runic energy is found in the spine. Here, both genders have a full set of 24 runes anchored in their very bones. We will look at spines and the entire nervous system as well as its extension into the energy body (Hamr) and beyond in its own dedicated work.

    A quick note is due. Even though women do lack the ᚩ Óðal (Othala) rune (and hence Y chromosome) by default, they do acquire it temporarily when they are pregnant with a male child[47] or when they acquire it from the semen of their male partners (more on this at a later point in time). It persists for many years before their bodies process it out. This is what makes women fall so deeply in love with their partners and makes separation of sex and love so difficult. It is also what causes mothers to bond so deeply with their sons until the maturation (and the son's bond with their mothers!). This also accounts for the difficulty in separation once the son has grown and is ready to start his own family. That process completes once the Y chromosome (and ᛟ Óðal (Othala)'s influence) fades out of the mother's body completely. It is also interesting to make a parallel observation in the social structure of old days, where a woman was told that she only achieved completeness as a woman once she became a mother. Could this have been a social understanding of these genetic influences? Or might it have only been, as many would believe, a way to control women's influence in society? Hard to discern the true motivation in these situations. It also goes to explain well why the Völva and Seiðr women in Norse culture were not solitary or celibate – for them, sex featured very prominently in their work. It was the acquisition of the Y chromosome from their male sexual partners which gave them the power to anchor their influences in the here and now (that is what ᛟ Óðal (Othala) does energetically).

    From the male, we gain the positive side of the runic energies and from the female, we gain the negative. They attract each other until they meet, and this, ladies and gents, is how the human double helix is formed. It is this energetic attraction of the plus and minus in runic energies which triggers the bonding of the initial strands which eventually form the double helix we are so familiar with in our DNA.

We need to be careful when we attach specific interpretations and meanings to DNA because our understanding of it keeps evolving. For instance, in 2013, scientists found that there are two codes in our genome, or to be more precise, that some of the genetic 'letters' or codes have two meanings with two completely 'new' separate functions (one controls the genes and the other the protein production with the two evoking in concert with each other). In effect, they have discovered the duality in the DNA which to the Rune Mystic would be the above-mentioned positive and negative runic influences. This is important to keep in mind. Human understanding of all this is evolving and should never be taken as fact or absolute. It is only ever understanding at a certain point in time, and as that point of time moves forward, understanding changes and reshapes itself constantly.

In addition to this, what is typically termed 'junk' DNA or non-encoding DNA by science is what holds a lot of the energetic coding for the energy systems of the physical body (Lik). This is why non-encoding DNA does not encode any proteins. That would be a physical function, and these parts of the genetic code are not meant for the physical (well not all of them, in any case) but for the energetic side. It is partly due to their action that we get the personalised life essence discussed in the blood section above (see 'Blood and "Personalised" Life Force'). This is also the part of the genetic information we target with rune work in order to activate its energetic functions. Once done, it will propagate along the entire genome in your physical body (Lik), awakening and changing what was dormant in a balanced and harmonised way.

Vibrating the DNA with Megin

Causing the DNA to vibrate and be enlivened with actual power (Megin) was discussed in 'Personification of the Hamingja' and 'Awakening the Breath of Oðin'.[48] It is well worth revisiting those practices and re-doing them a couple of times before moving onto the next ones.

The Blood of Lóðurr Awakens

Sól (Sowilo) DNA Activation

It is now time to move beyond vibrating the DNA or using it to personalise Megin as we have learnt to do in *The Breath of Oðin Awakens*. What the following practice does is activate the beneficial dormant memories, abilities, skills and powers in our DNA as well as physiologically beneficial characteristics. It will also make the physical body (Lik) ready to act as the foundation for the rest of the Self – or its anchor, if that concept fits your liking better. It is from the physical that we rise, and all those in human bodies are born out of the merging of flesh and spirit where either spirit forms flesh (otherwise conceptualised as descending into flesh, for those who are directionally oriented) or spirit is formed because of flesh (here, the flesh gives rise to the spirit). The latter is very rare – so much so that you have probably one or two cases in the whole of human history, hence no point wasting time on that here.

Start by relaxing and allowing the world to fade from your awareness. There is no need for a full trance state to do this. Simply relax and clear your mind for a few minutes. Focus on your body, feel the flesh of your very Being. Become aware of your blood flowing through your system, of the air you breathe joining that flow and how they give life to everything they come in contact with within you. Awaken your biological awareness and intend it to connect you with the DNA in each and every cell of your body. These two steps are important and are a key we did not have when working with DNA in *The Breath of Oðin Awakens*, though now we do (if you have not covered them, check the relevant chapters).

As usual, keep a clear mind and avoid imagining or anticipating anything. Your biological awareness will directly communicate things to your conscious awareness in the best manner for you personally. Once it does, you will experience something 'pop' into your mind. It will be an image or sensation which interrupts or is superimposed on whatever you have been thinking (or better yet, interrupt the silence in your mind if you use that instead, which is the ideal way to do it). Once that impression or perception to be more accurate 'pops into mind', you need to keep it in focus. Vocalise the ᛋ Sól (Sowilo) rune and its expansive white light with a pushing outwards sensation and slightly electric feel to it. It is an all-pervasive light which flows through everything, no matter what level of reality it is on, what density of matter it is, what type of energy it is and so forth. The light will simply flow through it and as it makes contact with it and changes it. This is exactly what we want. You will intend that this ᛋ Sól (Sowilo) light activates and awakens all the BENEFICIAL characteristics in your DNA. Here, you can be as specific or broad as you desire. You can intend only powers, abilities, or skills to be awoken, and you can intend those awake to be empowered and hyper-activated (excellent to do when trying to enhance your senses, by the way! Highly recommended!), or you can use the broad general awakening.

Always remember to focus in on the beneficial parts of it, because our DNA has non-beneficial parts as well as all sorts of other things that have been artificially made and folded into the human DNA patterns, which you definitely do not want! Focus on your intent and intend to grow and be benefited. Focus on what you intend to awaken, feel the DNA responding, feel it flaring up with ᛋ Sól (Sowilo) light and vibrating stronger and faster. You cannot do this for another or 'copy' things from others. You can only affect yourself, but there is so much treasure locked within each of us that there is ample potential for growth, development and experience within us without bothering with anyone else's DNA.

You will experience an energy rush if this is done right. It will either be a burst or a softer but longer-term flow of energy. Either way, you have succeeded in unleashing what you have aimed for. The next thing to do is to simply spend a few minutes visualising yourself fully with all sensory faculties active in using those abilities and skills and powers, or possessing those characteristics you have just intended to awaken.

When done, open your eyes and return to your daily activities. It is important to note that here, do not will the ᛋ Sól (Sowilo) energies to fade. Just forget about them and your biological awareness will maintain or fade them when it decides to do so. Typically, it maintains them for as long as it can and allows them to fade once it tires out or gets overwhelmed. Either way, that is exactly what you want. Here, you will not only awaken dormant DNA, but you are also teaching your conscious mind as well as your biological awareness to work together and rely on each other. You are building an even closer partnership between the two, which is absolutely essential for later work and advancement.

Quick Steps

1 Relax and allow your mind to clear of the daily hustle and bustle.
2 Become aware of the blood flowing through you (which by now should be familiar), of the air you breathe in and the life flowing through you. Connect with your biological awareness (see 'Biological Awareness' section above) and intend it to connect you with the DNA within.
3 Wait for the biological awareness to communicate. Avoid trying to anticipate it, to imagine what the DNA would be like, or to visualise anything. It is a matter of patiently waiting with a clear and receptive mind. When it does, it will simply 'pop into your mind', and it could be an image, a sensation or any other manner in which it chooses to do so. When you have it, focus in on it.
4 Vocalise the ᛋ Sól (Sowilo) rune, feel its expansive, all-pervasive, blinding light energy flow throughout the DNA. Quickening and activating it. What it activates will depend on what you intend. Be careful to select cautiously. You can pick an ability, a skill, a potential, a memory (yes, DNA encodes those too), some ancestral knowledge and so forth. Here the trick is to be specific.

Awakening random things in one's DNA is not a good idea. You have been warned.

5   Focus on what you intend to awaken. Feel the DNA responding, feel it flaring up with ᛋ Sól (Sowilo) light and vibrating stronger and faster.

6   Once you feel the energy rush from this activation, visualise yourself using the skill or ability sought, remembering the memories you want or having the potential you are trying to awaken. This is the key to grounding things into the flesh and hence reality.

7   When done, simply return to your typical daily activities and allow the energy to be dissipated by your biological awareness (not your conscious mind – DNA is its domain, not your mind's).

- The Blood of Lóðurr Awakens -

INTENT

Mastering Intent – Part II

It is now time to look at the second part of intent. We have seen in *The Spirit of Húnir Awakens – Part 2* that intent requires what is called pure thought, or otherwise language, image, sound and sensation-less thought, or pure impulse.[49]

Once that has been mastered, you will be one third of the way to full mastery of intent – well actually, more like half way there. The second part is sensation. In order to unleash intent, you will need bodily sensation to be fused with the pure thought. Combined, these two form actual intent and are the basis for intent-driven consciousness and actions. This is also the basis of creation and runic Galdr as well as the key requirement for a lot of Seiðr.

Gaining the sensory element of intent is a bit of a tricky one but not really difficult. The first step involves feeling the entire body. Just relax, still yourself and feel your body, letting your awareness of the sensations of the body flood your thoughts. Having gained a good solid sensing of the physical body, unleash your pure thought into it and allow it to merge with the body's sensations. For instance, intend to calm the physical systems in your body. Your intent is calm relaxation and peacefulness – or if you prefer, stillness. Once you have that as a pure thought, sense your body.

Having gained a solid sense of your body, allow the pure thought of calmness to flood your entire body and merge with your sense of it. For those who have a keen sense of perception, a change in the type of bodily sensation will take place and be more than noticeable. Allow this new intent sensation to flood every single cell of your body, to merge with it. When your entire physiology is sensing and responding to that intent-fuelled sense (in harmony with it), simply allow your biological awareness to flood you and you will have actual intent. You will see them merge, the sensations of intent arising in your physical body (Lik) and the biological awareness, and this fusion – or rather, the result of it – is actual intent. You should not worry too much about understanding it logically. All that is required are the sensations. This part of intent is purely physiological and sensory.

It may seem a long, tedious process, but the more you practice, the faster and easier it gets. The initial problem is simply that people seldom really intend, because they do not know how to, or even that it is possible to do. It is the same situation as a child learning to walk – damn hard work if you ask the child, but an automatic no-challenge act, if you ask the adult. This is exactly the same, because intent is actually unleashed by the body, not the mind. In time, it will be a matter of simply:

  1 Getting the pure thought of what is to be intended

2. Allowing the physiological sensation of that intent to be unleashed as directed by the will.
3. Unleashing your biological awareness and allowing it to flood the mix of pure thought flowing through the respective bodily sensations.

Very fast and simple. You should not worry about it for now. Simply focus on mastering the individual stages. For those of you who are following this closely, you will now realise just why the physical body (Lik) is so critically important in terms of spiritual evolution. Without learning to unleash intent, it would be a great challenge very few could achieve, if not impossible.

The Blood of Lóðurr Awakens

Mastering Intent – Part III

This is more of an application or extension of intent, rather than mastery thereof. Once you have a good grasp of unleashing it as a single event, the next stage is to stream it as a flow. This simply requires you intending to intend as a flow of whatever you are aiming to intend. How is that for a mind loop! Start off with your intent, then get to the point where you have the sensation of all your cells in your body sensing the intent and unleashing it. The result of this is that the intent which is initiated as pure thought in your mind – an impulse of pure thought – is then felt by every cell in your body (in other words, the full extent of your biological awareness). This amplifies and condenses it, and then you unleash it. At that moment, you initiate a second flow of the same intent and bring it to the point where the cells are in harmony with the sensing of that second intent. Simply unleash them both at the same time. Job done! The original intent will flow as a stream of willed intent. Their energy should fuse into a single streaming wave of intending until you willingly turn it off or run out of power. A simple 'enough' or 'stop' thought does the trick. This is called 'Streaming of Intent' or 'Intending'. The two labels can be used interchangeably, although the former gives a slightly better understanding of the process for the logical mind.

Quick Steps

1 Start as usual with your intent. Ensure every cell in your body feels it and is echoing the intent (in effect, your biological awareness is intending, alongside your conscious mind). Then unleash it.
2 As you unleash intent, make sure you also intend that unleashed intent to flow (think of it as streaming the intent, if that helps).
3 Then start the process once more through points 1 and 2, and when the cells of your body are vibrating with this second wave, release it alongside the first. Their energy should fuse into a single streaming wave of intending until you willingly turn it off or run out of power. A simple 'enough' or 'stop' thought does the trick.

As usual, practice makes perfect. A master of intending can unleash waves upon waves of intending in such a rapid stream of pure willed awareness that even trying to time it in a matter of one second would be infinitely too slow. Naturally, for the runic work at hand, there is simply no need for that level of intending proficiency. Simply unleashing a single intent will do the trick nicely –, if possible, mastering the streaming of that one intent would be very helpful as well, but beyond that, we are looking at applications which are simply far too advanced for the matter at hand.

Pulling The Self into The Lik

This is where our approach in Norse mysticism differs significantly from practically all other traditions. We bring the higher parts of the Self INTO the physical, rather than seek to escape the physical by merging with the higher. In other words, those parts of the Self become part of our physical and conscious domain. The physical body (Lik) becomes the centre point for all the rest.

The next stage of the practice involves going a step further and bringing into the physical (Lik) all the embodiments of the Self. This includes all other personas we build over the course of our lives, all the perceptions of Self we have (us the parent, us the child, us the husbands, us the wives, us the professional, us the 'whatever your job may be', us the embodiments in our dreams and so forth). All these temporary glimpses of self-embodiment are brought into the physical body (Lik) and merged into biological and conscious awareness.

Some will wonder why on earth we use this approach, rather than just seeking to merge out of the physical into the so-called 'higher' parts of the Self. This is for two reasons: one is that the so-called 'higher' parts of the Self are not necessarily higher at all, we only label them as such because they are perceived as being more 'mysterious' and hence more 'exalted' than our normal consciousness. The other is that our personality – and hence, the main expression of our individuality at this point in time – is rooted in the physical body (Lik). We know that when we die, this will dissipate and our Self partly fades and partly returns to the essence type of expression, and remerges with either the ancestral, or other manifestations in creation (such as a descendant for the Hugr, if gifted). This means that you will essentially no longer have a 'complete' Self as you do at this point in time. Hence the teachings on Midgard being the centre of creation, and us children of Midgard being centres of the Self provide us with a unique opportunity to complete our Selves.

Since the main part of the Self which is responsible for the conscious awareness we have – and hence our personality – is the physical body (Lik), that is our main focus. We bring all that which we can into the physical (Lik) and into the reach of our conscious awareness, rather than losing ourselves by merging into so-called 'higher' forms of expression, which in turn, will have to embody again in a new Self and repeat the cycle until completion (which does include the physical – you cannot complete a whole if you persistently reject one of its parts) is achieved. Some will argue that this is re-incarnation, but it is not. Reincarnation is a concept where 'you' are reborn again to live life anew. But if parts of 'you' are actually dissolved and lost, or flow into another, it is no longer the 'you' that you are. It will be some other form of you, with a new form of consciousness, a new personality and a new expression of the individuality. It is exactly like changing a molecule in a chemical – even the slightest alteration produces a completely new and hence different molecule. This new 'you' is no longer the same, and is no longer 'you'. This new personality is, technically speaking, someone else with your intellect and experiences and abilities as a starting point for which it builds its own Self. 'Yours' is dissipated and some of its parts have been reused.

    This, ladies and gents, completes our initial foundational work with the physical body (Lik) and puts us in great standing to being our energy body (Hamr) work. Needless to say, what you have worked through in these few chapters is the tip of the iceberg, but is an essential start. More exciting things to discover? Always. We never end our learning and just as we think we have a solid knowledge of things, we realise that we have only breached the threshold. Fun, is it not?

- The Blood of Lóðurr Awakens -

THE ENERGY BODY (HAMR)

Energy Body (Hamr)
Fundamentals

Many different cultures share many different views on what we have come to call, in our modern area, the 'energy body' – also referred to in a more traditional context as the human soul. Because of the 'globalistic' nature of knowledge sharing, this has more often than not resulted in a mish-mash and horrible blending of what one can term the spaghetti-understanding of the topic. In addition, we have the problem of variations in the fundamental structures of the energy body (Hamr) dependent on gender, race, ancestral heritage and so forth. The overriding conception of the energy body (Hamr) being just that – a body of energy resulting in the assumption that this structure of the Self will always be alike for everyone – is a critical misconception. Existence values individualisation and the entire evolutionary drive is to produce as many unique and individual life forms as possible. As a matter of energetic fact, if two or more energy bodies (Hamur) were the same, they would fuse into a single one. The more alike one is to the other, the more their boundaries merge, according to the law of *like attracting like*.

This unfortunately means that in order to gain an in-depth knowledge of your energy body (Hamr) and its underlying capabilities, you will need to go and search through the original teachings of whichever racial background you come from and look at what those teachings provide, in terms of specific information with regard to your energetic heritage. A quick note on gender: the energy body (Hamr) will always match the natural biological gender which you have been born. Unfortunately, there is no surgery or treatment available to change that, other than creating a new energy body (Hamr) and replacing the existent one. As you can imagine, a feat still well beyond the capabilities of most.

As far as inherited characteristics, you can easily discover those from various stories your parents and grandparents tell you about various members of your family. These are critically important in discovering how your ancestors have shaped future generations' energy bodies (souls or Hamur).

Because it is impossible to enter into all these details, some of which are so personal that it would be impossible to put in a book, we will look at the generic characteristics of an energy body instead. The trick to apply when delving into the more specific areas is to remember that the runes were inscribed upon ALL things (and also life forms) in creation. It matters not what gender, race or ancestry you come from, as they will all be there (with the exception of ᛟ Óðal (Othala)). The Jarls have an additional set of three runes in their energy bodies, but since we are not going to look at those, all the information in here applies to everyone!

The Cycle of Existence of The Hamr

When you ask most, defining the energy body (or even the soul) seems to be very problematic. Everyone seems to have some form of unconscious grasp of it, but when it comes into the realm of mind and logic (Hugr), almost everyone struggles to pinpoint its nature or function. This is not surprising, purely due to the fact that as far as the complete structure of the Self is concerned the mind/intellect (Hugr) is not directly connected to the energy body (Hamr) – it has to go through the Spirit (Óðr) which is connected to the physical body (Lik), and then through the body (Lik) (via biological awareness) to the energy body (Hamr). In other words, it traverses a type of maze through the structures of the Self to even get to the energy body (Hamr), let alone start to analyse and learn about it. Additionally, the second point of difficulty arises from the fact that the Hamr is a body of energy and understands (or interacts) with things in terms of pure energy, it is a 'fluid' body. Hence, when dealing with it, there is a complete total lack of terms of interpretation and understand which our minds need to in order to learn about it. However, having worked through *The Spirit of Húnir Awakens - Parts 1 & 2* and through the biological awareness practices (and hopefully the Hamingja ones too in *The Breath of Oðin Awakens*), your mind should be able to start interacting with this level of reality without having to have recourse to logic or be limited by linguistics. Always leave the interpretation of your experiences until AFTER the entire experience has been experienced! And be aware that your interpretation and understanding of these will change as your scope of conscious awareness grows. As discussed above, we also have the problem of people assuming the energy system of the physical body (Lik) as being the energy body (Hamr) itself to contend with.

Birth of The Hamr

The birth of an energy body (Hamr) is one of the most fascinating topics you can encounter. Why so? Because it relates directly to the basic shapes of creation. Everything in existence, in energetic terms, is structured into very basic geometric shapes. For instance, human beings tend to be spheres of energy (think the shape of your auric field as being a bubble that is the shape of your energy body or soul). Other forms of consciousness adopt other basic shapes depending on their nature.

This little conceptual diversion will help you understand the basic shared nature of all Hamur. In the case of human beings, when the Fylgja finds descendants with a suitable genetic basis, it will attach to the foetus as soon as the sperm breaks through the wall of the egg. This is when life actually begins. **The sperm carries the seed of life and the egg provides it with the environment in which to grow and germinate.** When the sperm breaches the wall of the egg on the energetic level, an explosion of luminosity occurs (scientists have found this to be the case physically as well, due to the explosion of zinc[50]). This event sends energetic waves down the ancestral lines which signal to all dormant Fylgjur that a newborn is being formed. Whichever Fylgja resonates best with the totality of genetics in the foetus will be attracted to it. It is a type of magnetic pull (on the energetic and spiritual levels) which seeds the Fylgja into the foetus. At this point, the foetus has a Spirit on the archetypal level. As the two interact with each other, the Fylgja customises whatever genetics it needs (a process very similar to epigenetics turning DNA on or off) but in this case, it not only acts on the DNA, which has physical modes of expression (such as hair colour, skin types, eye colour and so forth), but also on genetics which impact the rest of the Self on the energetic and mental levels of existence (hence things such as memories, intellect, energy body structures, powers and abilities, preferences in all things physical AND energetic, as well as mental and so forth). Once all of this is set, it makes a connection to the source of life which brought it form (in other words, through the initial seed cells of the sperm) to the father's ancestral lines. From there, a complex interchange will occur, supervised by the kin-Fylgja (ancestral spirit) where access to the ancestral pools of power (Megin) and ancestral Ørlǫg (personal/ancestral fate) are drawn up, and if this is the firstborn male of the new generation, then the kin-Fylgja seeds itself in the foetus.

In cases where the kin-Fylgja seeds itself in the child, it then makes changes to the genetic expression similar to those made by the Fylgja. And yes, it can override those changes made by the Fylgja. This is because the first-born male gradually, over his lifetime, becomes a host for the ancestral and/or tribal spirit's (the kin-Fylgja) full embodiment. This shifting of the ancestral Fylgja is initiated at the point of conception and is an ongoing preparation until the death of the father. At that point, the full and complete kin-Fylgja removes itself from the father and hosts itself in the eldest son. If you look closely at those individuals, you will see how character changes occur. With kin-Fylgja which are very ancient, these changes can result in a very different person to what the eldest son was before. The process is fascinating to observe as this spirit weaves itself into the Y-Chromosome and seeds itself throughout his biology, by spreading through this chromosome across his entire physiology.

At this point – or in some cases, where the individual has a special purpose just before this point – the Wyrd (universal or 'big picture' aspect of fate) starts to interact with the energy systems more thoroughly than before. It sets up the directionality of the entire energy system, the intensity of its flow and the blockages which that child will have to work through in his or her lifetime. These are in addition to all the challenges to be faced as instigated from the ancestral Ørlọg (think of it as personal fate, or ancestral fate resulting from the Self, rather than the 'Cosmic big picture' one as dictated by Wyrd). We will look more closely at the whole 'fate' influences (or lack thereof) on various stages of birthing and existence of the Self at a later point in time.

Once this whole business is over and the genetics are all primed, as Megin starts to flow through them (in order to activate them), the Hamingja becomes apparent and cell division occurs (the growth of the foetus is initiated). This is the point where the Hamr (soul) is formed, just before the very first division and right after the genetic imprinting (the spirit(s) linking fully into the foetus) that the blueprint nature of the Hamr is established. All the 'programming' for each and every cell in this human being and his or her future is set. It is also at this point that the spherical shape of the Hamr gains a concentration of energy (and information) in its very centre. The shaping on the inner part of the Hamr is complete and it becomes part of a fully functional soul for the individual. This causes your energy body (Hamr) to adapt to the sphere shape WITHIN, which contains a fully formed you. Human awareness takes root at its most basic fundamental level. For the mother, she experiences a 'glow' – an additional radiance in her

Self because she has two energy bodies within (hers and the child's). On the other hand, it is at this point that her Self has to provide energy for two. We will go into how this all happens elsewhere because the division of the Spark of Self, where the father loses half of his and the mother loses a quarter of hers, happens at an archetypal level and not the energetic.

By this stage, we have a fully functional Hamr to work from. As it grows (in terms of energy not structure – the structure is set by now), so does the physical. Things do not stop there. The Fylgja (and if appropriate, the kin-Fylgja) remain very busy ensuring the development of the child. It is during this process that the shadow (Sal) is both established and grows in direct proportion to the physical (Lik) and energy body (Hamr) growth. The pattern is easy to follow: you have impulse for growth + energy/power in the Hamr, which then is reflected in the shadow (Sal) and they cause growth in the physical (at this point, it would be cell division). These impulses are generated by those Fylgjur and their interactions with the genetics in the child. This answers the bafflingly simplistic question of 'when does the life of a child start?' It starts at the moment after the sperm breaches the wall of the egg, causing all these spiritual and ancestral mechanisms to kick into action.

Death of the Hamr

If you think the birth of the energy body (Hamr) was complicated, wait until you start looking into its death – or to be more accurate, its dissolution process! We will not go into as much detail on this topic because there is no need to do so in the context of this work.

When a person dies physically, it triggers a whole range of events on the energetic level of the Self (mostly due to the fact that the physical, being the apex of this level of Self for most people, is suddenly no longer functioning!). Both the energy body (Hamr) and shadow (Sal) are dependent on not only physical functioning but also on the energies it provides and on its mechanisms, which support conscious awareness. Suddenly, the energy body (Hamr) finds itself free of the gravity of physical energy, which no longer has any pull and can no longer keep various parts together and cohesive. When death strikes for those we shall call 'typical people' (in other words, those who have not yet successfully integrated their Self completely and those who have created no additional Hamr), the energy body (Hamr) splits off from the physical, and so does the shadow (Sal), because the energetic relationship between the shadow (Sal) and energy body (Hamr) was based on the support of physical life that is now broken too. The energy body (Hamr), being the second-best host for consciousness, has the latter jump into it for a 'ride'. Unfortunately, since the energy body (Hamr) lacks cohesion or substance (it is pure energy), it can only maintain consciousness for a limited amount of time. Additionally, due to the fact that awareness requires vast amounts of energy to function, the energy body (Hamr) has separated from the physical with no connection left to draw energy from, and starts to run out of energy. It also finds itself in an environment where energy is a valuable commodity and very scarce (in terms of free energy). Most typical persons fail to provide a viable long-term source to fuel their Hamr, so over a short space of time, depending on how full its reserves are, it will run depleted. As soon as it does, it will start to fade. This is what traditionally was termed 'the second death' – in effect, it is the dissolution of the Hamr (soul or energy body). At that point, consciousness and awareness have no more energy to run on. The Spirit (Óðr) picks up what it needs from it and then proceeds to reintegrate with the Spark of Self. Unless the Spark of Self has been grown, it too will in time, without any additional targets of expression of its Self, diminish until all is left is the essence of that very Spark, eventually returning to the Gap (nothingness). The shadow (Sal), on the other hand, is an embodiment of instinct and tries to latch onto whatever it can. This is where all the 'ghost' stories come from and why all these ghosts are actually bound to their 'places' on earth and so forth. Eventually, they are reabsorbed by the Earth itself as fuel for its growth.

It is important to understand that this is an outline of the process. In most people who are still plagued by the 'Mind Thief' (see *The Spirit of Húnir Awakens – Part 1*), their energy body (Hamr) will be dragged up into the collective of this entity as it tries to disassociate itself from its human host (food source). This is where the experiences of going up to heaven – and seeing the lights at the end of the tunnels and so forth – come from. Once on the 'other side', where the mind thief is completely separated from the human, energy body (Hamr) and consciousness are thrown back and undergo their normal dissolution process(es). In these cases, because of the theft of energy, the dissolution is far more rapid. Those of a 'typical' person usually last from three days to three months. Those with a lot of spare energy can drag it on for much longer – in some cases, even up to three years. But eventually, all dissolve. You will know when the dissolution has reached near completion stage when people start to forget about their deceased loved ones. The memories fade and their presence is no longer as tangible as it was closer to the time of death.

When without physical bodies (Lik) to anchor the individual into Midgard, the energy body (Hamr) is thrown out (its natural place is no longer Midgard after all). This is when the energy body/soul starts to journey onto Helheim, which becomes its new home. Due to the energy deficit, everything slows down, becomes harder and even more challenging. This matches the arduous trips described in the Eddas and the multiple references to slowness in Hellia's realm. Unlike in fiction (and most movies), all things dead are slow – it is their nature as they are in effect on a transitional phase from stasis to nothingness (complete dissolution). One way to 'escape' this is to anchor one's energy body (Hamr) into another universe or being. We will look at this at a later point in time. Another is to expand the rays of Self into a new energy body (Hamr), after integration of the Self, and embody them fully in the other six worlds. This actually does happen in Midgard (on Earth), a good example being the Dalai Lama's so called 'reincarnation' where a new energy body (Hamr) is hosted in a young child.

This is why there is actually no reincarnation, which is just a modern concept to make people feel good about there not being an end to their end. They all end. It is only the essence of experiences and memories which are preserved by the Fylgjur for the next generation and the essence of their power preserved by their Hamingjur. In these cases, the Self has existed, it has manifested and experienced life but has failed to germinate (remember, it is a seed trying to grow within what is called the physical level of reality). What it has gained (experiences, memories and power) is preserved, while the rest simply dissipates along with it in order to leave room for the next generation, which will make us from all that the previous generations have contributed, in its own attempt to grow and germinate. Simple, effective and clean.

Having said all of this, for atypical individuals who have fully formed a totally cohesive and integrated Self, the 'death' events are totally different. In those rare ones, when the physical body (Hamr) dies, the full breadth, scope and potential of their biological awareness shifts into their energy body (Hamr). This gives the energy body (Hamr) an incredible level of cohesion. With this, the energy gravity from the physical is now gained by the energy body (Hamr). This in turn pulls the shadow (Sal) in, and suddenly you find yourself with a 'body' which has both substance and energy, mass and gravity (sounds familiar? Very much like what the physical is). This new body is subtler than the physical but sits on the borderline of energy density, just in between the pure energy and the physical energy levels. With sufficient progress, the energy body (Hamr) will have learnt how to draw on the essence of physicality and start to act as a proper body would. This makes it just as ideal a vehicle for conscious awareness as the physical was. With its energetic gravity resulting from large energy reserves, there is no problem in maintaining awareness until new sources of 'food' (energy) are found (if not already established beforehand). The very structure of the energy body (Hamr) changes and gains a brilliance, running throughout ALL its energy and shape. Naturally adapting to the new 'environment' takes time, but at least you have a body which can do so. What happens to such individuals is effectively a flipping of the triangle of Self upside down, where now at the apex you have the energy body (Hamr) and at the bottom you have the shadow (Sal) and Physical levels (where pure biological awareness replaces the actual physical body itself).

At this point, the entire Self starts to express other characteristics and powers, a new form of awareness unfolds (which is typically dormant during physical life).

There are many other scenarios which are part and parcel of these two end death processes. What you have here is the 'typical person' and the fully integrated Self person scenarios. There are many between these two which have various degrees of the one and the other. It is best to think of these as fluctuations being in between those two poles. Which you will undertake depends entirely on how far you have evolved during your lifetime and on how well you have prepared (and, to a certain extent, how you have prepared).

Hopefully, these few pages will suffice to give you a broad overview of what happens upon physical death. As for the death process itself, it is best conceptualised as a digression towards stasis. Life at the birth point is the highest point of anti-stasis you can get – activity is at its absolute peak there, and during youth. As you age, you start to lessen in activity (typically) and stasis starts to take hold. By the time of death (assuming an old-age death), stasis has a firm grip on you and has reached the point where there is so little activity that it drags you from physical energy decay to pure energetic decay (in other words, you die and your energy body (Hamr) starts its own decay process as the Self splits), with you eventually going on to Helheim, and there, you slow down to the point of being more and more subject to stasis, until eventually you sink further into the deeper depths of Niflheim, where either Níðhögg devours what is left or you sink into total complete stasis and are claimed by the Gap. This is what a 'typical' energetic view of death is. It is why the Eddas tell us that all those who die of old age and disease end up in Hella's domain (Helheim). All that we do in terms of evolution is to counter this process. Even the selected for Valhöll would undergo this but are able to shortcut this whole process by being taken to Valhöll, where they eat and drink of the foods of another world and prepare for battle (according to the Eddas). This is a reawakening of activity from stasis! Those given the Mead of Memory, through the functions of memory, regain cohesion and proceed to one of the higher worlds.

Before ending this discussion, it is worth taking note that not all 'typical people' always undergo this bleak view of things. Some are fortuned by Wyrd (fate) to encounter someone with a Divine Spark (extremely rare but it does happen). These individuals' Sparks of Self are infused with Archetypal Divinity in its highest forms of expression and are, for all intents and purposes, on energetic levels similar to Immortal Suns blazing divine brilliant light forth. What those people who encounter these individuals can experience is a type of pull into the orbit of those blazing suns. They become similar to what in planetary terms we would see as satellites orbiting those suns. The radiation of this divine brilliance then provides energy for the energy body (Hamr) of such individuals. This, in turn, gives them the opportunity to maintain conscious awareness and work on their evolution whilst being 'dead'. They become what, in the old days, we used to term 'living ones'. Not much else can be said on this because it is a great mystery which only those who share in it can understand. For our purposes, it is not really needed. All you need to get to grips with is the basic process of creation and dissipation of the energy body (Hamr) and Self.

The Hamr in Eddic and Traditional Sources

The energy body (Hamr)'s shape-giving characteristics were well known and acknowledged in the past – specifically, in all legends of Seiðr women's abilities to shapeshift by changing the initial shape of their Hamur[51] and by academics within the field.[52] Additionally, as we will see when dealing with topics of creation of additional Hamr (or sHamr)[53], these shaping characteristics were not only understood to determine the shapes of our physical forms and all forms of the immediate expression of Self, but also provided the ability of expanding on the scope of characteristics the Self could express at any single point in time via a sHamr (think of the sHamr as an additional energy body (Hamr) – we will look at these in great detail in due course).

We also have accounts of Hamr (and sHamr) being used for projection, where the physical body (Lik) was left behind by conscious awareness, using the Hamur as a vehicle. In such cases, the physical body (Lik) left behind would lose semblance of life (grow cold to the touch, become pale as if dead, have an incredibly slow heartbeat to the point where it seemed to no longer beat and so forth)[54]. We gain some interesting insights from such accounts which will be of use in later advanced practices, but are worth mentioning at this point in order to avoid leaving theoretical gaps in understanding.

For shapeshifting to occur, you need your mind to have an understanding or experiential essence of whatever it is you are going to shift into. In other words, some part of your needs to have lived in the shape you seek to adopt, and these experiences will need to be assimilated by the conscious, AND the physical body (Lik) needs to have a biological awareness of what it is like to function (or be) in the target form.[55] Additionally, you need to be able to perceive as a native Being of that form. Without those, shapeshifting cannot occur, as it would be seen as alien to the current Self and be rejected by one of its nine constituent parts. For instance, if you want to shapeshift into a bird, your mind (Hugr) would need to know how to think like a bird, how to perceive as one and how to be one. Your physical body (Lik) would need to know how to move as one, how to breathe as one, how to behave as one and so forth. The problem most have is that they can only relate to how 'they' think a bird would think and they can only conceive of how a bird would move by watching how a bird moves. That fails to capture any of the intricate detail(s) involved in the movement or thinking of a bird! The list of asynchonicity goes on to include each and every aspect of the Self-involved. Some who have strong Fylgjur can gain those insights directly from them, and it is not uncommon for those individuals to shapeshift into the forms of their Fylgja. The final component required for shapeshifting is a powerful Hamingja. The process, if one can achieve it, essentially involves acquiring all the knowledge and experiences outlined above, then using your mind (Hugr), forcing by its strength a new shape onto the energy body (Hamr), then using Megin (from the Hamingja) with intent to solidify it and impose a total change in shape, which results in the change of the blueprint (Hamr) and then propagates (providing sufficient power is available) on the shape of the physical body (Lik), for as long as there is sufficient Megin to maintain this new shape.

- The Blood of Lóðurr Awakens -

Energy Body Cohesion and Shaping

The energy body (Hamr) has no mass, it is fluid but without mass. It is energy without mass, unlike the physical body (Lik) which also has an energetic component and has mass. This is the fundamental distinction between the pure energy body (Hamr) and the physical body (Lik)'s energy structures and systems. Because the energy body (Hamr) has no mass, it has only minimal cohesion. This is also the reason why it has very few 'limits'. It can, for instance, shift itself from your current location into not only a completely different point in the universe, but also into a completely different time. There is no mass transference and hence there is no time limitation either.

Because of this lack of mass, it cannot maintain consciousness – or rather, to be more precise, our conscious awareness cannot use it as a vehicle for perception and is unable to function within it. In order to do so, we need to increase both the degree of cohesion and mass available to it. It is only once those conditions are satisfied that we can start awakening and using it as a vehicle for conscious perception. There are essentially two different methods to achieve this goal: one is the transference of the subtlest elements of what gives our physical bodies mass (biological awareness) and the other is by condensation of energy within the energy body (Hamr) itself. With the former, we are making the physical body that little bit less physical, but it is a much easier and quicker route to imbuing our energy bodies (Hamr) with the required mass and cohesion.

Additionally, since our conscious awareness is so used to inhabiting our physical bodies, it makes both the transference and the functioning (as well as the maintaining) of conscious awareness in the energy body (Hamr) so much easier to achieve. The limitation at play is that the shaping of the energy body (Hamr) has to be a complete, perfect match of the physical form (this also includes the energetic components of our physical bodies). With the latter, we form the energy body(Hamr)'s shape based on the energy type used to condense it (or concentrate it, if you prefer). Here, the form will rise spontaneously but will always be a symbolic representation of the Self and the energy type use. This gives us more flexibility but is a much, much, much longer process. Just how long? It can take more than a single lifetime to achieve.

The danger, too, is that because we are drawing on non-physical energy, we are also opening ourselves up to ALL the influences of that energy and all those who work with it. Let us put this into context. If you opt for the second method and use the energies of nature, you will be building your energy body's cohesion with that energy 'signature' – or typing, as it is usually called. That means all the forces of nature, and all those things which are linked to those energies of nature, be they positive or negative, helpful or harmful, will have a direct route of effecting you. Previously, they would not have – the virtue of being a physical biology locks all those things and influences out. By selecting a specific energy type to work with, you are opening yourself up to ALL those influences. Additionally, the key problem with doing this is that you are doing something akin to over-specialisation of your energy body (Hamr). For someone who uses their biological energy systems to bring mass and cohesion to their energy bodies (Hamur), they will have everything within the reach of the human awareness/domain available. Some might dismiss this, but it is worth keeping in mind humanity are the children of Midgard, the centre point where all energies of the Nine Worlds meet and meld. This gives us a massive pool of possibilities and energies to work with and an even larger array of permutations. If you were to count them, they would run into hundreds of thousands, if not more. All those are automatically available to us and those include the runic ones. Now compare that to someone who is specialising into one or two or three energies – see how limited they become in comparison? Their perceptions would, by the very nature of their forming energy bodies (Hamur), undergo the same limitations until eventually they would lose the very ability to perceive the fact that there are countless other possibilities – because for them, they would be encompassing all that is possible in their limited spectrum. This is one of the reasons why so many highly evolved forms of consciousness seek out the 'human experience' and undergo countless hardships in exchange for the potential of widening perception and the scope of their very Self.

Preparing The Energy Body for Use

The main problem with the energy body (Hamr) is that we have to reach it. What is meant by this is simple, yet very profound, in practical terms. It points to the fact that it is dormant and out of reach (typically), which is why a lot of people have no direct energy awareness. They fail to see it, fail to hear the sounds of its vibrations, fail to perceive the sensory information from it and so forth. The energy body (Hamr) is typically dormant due to two key factors, as detailed below.

The first of these is that the link from the Spirit (Óðr) is to the physical (Lik), so the standard perceived input is from physical reality. We are, in effect, constantly focussed on perceiving matter and being influenced by matter (Physicality) rather than perceiving energy and being influenced by it directly. The latter is gained from the energy body (Hamr) but for us to be able to use this body, we need to fuel it and keep it in an active state rather than dormant, undernourished and in quasi-stasis. The only way to give it drive is for the Spirit (Óðr) to link itself to the energy body (Hamr) and start perceiving from within it. This is harder to achieve than one thinks, because the Spirit (Óðr) is only ever linked directly to one of the other parts of the Self. It is also one of the reasons why, when projecting with the energy body (Hamr), which is what real astral projection is all about, the physical body (Lik) goes into a state of stasis resembling death. Breathing and the heartbeat reduce so much that unless you look very closely and know what to look for, it will appear as if the person projecting is actually dead. The skin turns a faint shade of blue/white and loses the colouring of normality and so forth. These are all symptoms of actual projection, or as we term it, ecstasy trance work, where the individual loses ALL awareness and perceptions of the physical.

The other main problem is fuelling the energy body (Hamr). It does get a background minimal amount of energy from sleep and biological food when digested by our physical bodies (Lik), but the totality of energy gained is nothing more than the bare absolute minimum. It does not gain any degree of additional energy to fuel activity or perception. Those who force its awakening without making additional energy available to fuel its activities find very rapidly that their lives start becoming flooded with problems, health issues, and things start going wrong left right and centre. This is simply due to the fact that the energy is being redirected from the personal stores into the energy body (Hamr) to fuel activity. Once those start to run out, it returns into a state of stasis, leaving you with a mess to fix in your daily life and other parts of the Self. This is why we need to fuel the energy body (Hamr) in various ways in order to not only provide it with the fuel it needs to awaken, but also on a constant basis for it to grow and expand in its activity. Its initial awakening will cause it to be an equivalent to a young child. Those little ones eat a lot of food! The same is true for our energy bodies (Hamr).

The Silver Cord

Having looked at the need for cohesion and structure within the energy body (Hamr), as previously mentioned in 'The Body (Lik), The Energy Body (Hamr) and Shadow (Sal)', the energy body (Hamr) overlaps the physical and is linked with it by thin, elastic-like energy substance threads. These threads are what people often refer to as the 'silver cord' they see when projecting. This is formed from the millions upon millions of tiny threads linking every part of the physical with the energetic (remember the former provides energy to the latter). When you try to project the energy body (Hamr), it pulls all those threads outwards. They coalesce at their central point of tension (the bellybutton area), thus forming the silver cord which is projected outwards from the

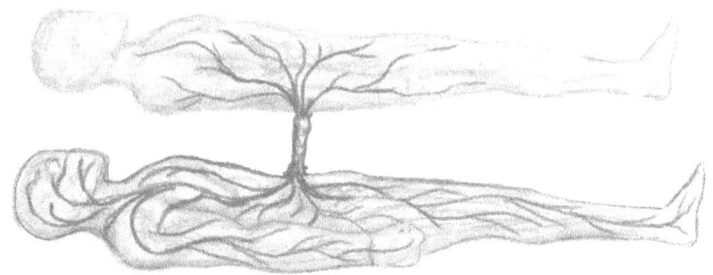

Silver Cord structure when projecting

navel (bellybutton) into the central area of the energy body (Hamr).

Shape of The Hamr

When working with the Hamr, it is always important to remember that its outer boundaries are in fact the Outer Boundary of your entire auric field. That is the shape of your energy body (Hamr) at the root level – it is a sphere and only its central portion takes on the shape of your body, but all the energy within the sphere IS the actual energy body (Hamr). Because of our socially indoctrinated obsession with physicality and physical bodies (Lik), part of this energy body (Hamr) condenses in the same space as we find the physical. Over generations, this phenomenon has resulted in changes to the energy body (Hamr), where its point of centrality shifted into a type of fluid shape within the physical, where it subsequently concentrated its energy produced and the 'core' you feel as the layer immediately under your skin. This layer under your skin is where our awareness is limited to. As you can imagine, this is a very small portion of the energy body (Hamr). This is part of the reason why so little of the energy reality is perceived. Perception of this part of reality is dependent on the functions of the energy body (Hamr), which in turn is dependent on our awareness and how far it extends into the energy body (Hamr).

Whilst talking about the energy body(Hamr)'s shape, it is important to keep in mind that in some rare cases, certain individuals do have different basic shapes to their energy body (Hamr). They are never very different from the basic sphere: they can be egg shaped, spheres with straight vertical sides and so forth. Essentially, they are all permutations of the basic spherical shape. It is, however, important if you sense yours to be one of these permutations, you follow that shape rather than trying to forcefully conform to the standard one.

Intending The Hamr

Gaining the understanding of intent and intending has opened up the possibility of formation of the energy body (Hamr). The energy body (Hamr) is the carrier of information. This is why we often term the energy body (Hamr) as a body, because it has energy and information, hence shape – but it is not the shape of the physical. In some, it is a set of two or more of these shapes, although this is extremely rare. In order to shape it for consciousness, we need to intend it from within the physical.

This is why mastering the streaming of intent was beneficial and important. Once you have the ability to generate intent, you can start reshaping the Hamr in order to allow it to host your conscious awareness. It will then become an actual energy body, for all intents and purposes. What needs to be done is simple: unleash either a series of individual intents on a regular basis or a stream of intending that your energy body (Hamr) becomes. You are forming the Hamr. This will have to be done over a longer period of time, because it has a tendency to default back to a mass of energy. Additionally, you will have to pour as much energy into it as possible, not only for this shaping but also for its cohesion and stability. We will look at hyper-shaping later on. For now, these basics should be used as often as possible. Doing so will strengthen your intent work AND will make the entire energy body (Hamr) more and more accessible to conscious influence, until eventually it will become a fully-fledged host for it. At a later point, we will look at how using the other parts of the Self and eventually merging them into the energy body (Hamr) can unlock a total complete Self. One step at a time.

We spend so much time being aware of the physical body (Lik), practically every instant of our waking life, time to spend more and more time intending the energy body (Hamr). The more awareness you pour into it, the more your awareness will shift from the purely physical into the energetic. Eventually, since the physical body (Lik) is already fully formed and functioning, it needs limited awareness and hence limited energy, unlike the energy body (Hamr). The idea is to shift as much to the energy body (Hamr) as possible. As it gains the ability to host your conscious awareness, so too does it provide an extremely wide set of perceptive tools for you to take advantage of. Eventually, you become able to maintain both switching between one and the other at will.

This is why there is no point doing actual Galdr work before having worked on at least this part of the Self. Filling a mass of energy with runic energy will just cause it to dissipate, leaving no concentration sufficient to achieve anything. By forming the energy body (Hamr) properly, you are also building a container for runic power which can then be used to direct and manipulate that energy, rather than just allowing it to dissipate.

Remember to focus on the depth of the body when intending the energy body (Hamr). All too often, we only focus on the surface of the body, skin, or back and immediate muscle under that. However, we forget to intend the depth of our bodies, the bones, the internal organs – that entire dimension of being needs to be included in our intending the energy body (Hamr).

Empowered with Intent

Once you have gained basic mastery of intending the energy body (Hamr), it is time to move on from simply intending the energy body (Hamr) to intending each and every action/movement you make in the physical body (Lik) whilst SIMULTANEOUSLY intending it in the energy body (Hamr). For instance, if you want to get up and make a coffee, you are intending in your energy body (Hamr), so you unleash the intent to get up, then an intent to move to the kitchen and so forth. As you release the intent, allow IT to drive the physical body (Lik) movements. Eventually, you will get to the point where you do not need to be consciously aware of your physical movement – all you do is unleash the intent of where you want to be and allow your energy body (Hamr) to move the physical for you. Take this slowly; it is one of those annoyingly frustrating and slow learning curves, but every second of effort you put into it will yield significant results in these and later far more complex practices. The rewards are most definitely worth each ounce of effort put into it.

Perceiving the Energy Body (Hamr)

It is important to practice sensing your energy body (Hamr) before trying to work with it. This sensing will allow you to expand your biological awareness further into and throughout the energy body (Hamr). It also prepares the energy body (Hamr) for future blending with the other parts of the Self, which is essential in mastering and knowing the Self!

Start by siting with your hands on your legs (quads). Sit perfectly still and just breathe, relax and still your mind. Let the tension fade away whilst keeping your thoughts from rambling on. Instead, focus on how your body feels. Once you are in a relaxed state of mind (and hence, a slight trance), shift your awareness to your skin. Feel the energy pulsating on

Trance & meditation (sitting) position

and through it, dancing on its surface. Having established the feel of this, refocus on the fact that you are inside your skin. Feel all your outer physical body (Lik) as being a glove, which you are in. It is from this part of you, which is inside, from where this radiating pulse you feel pulsing steadily out of your skin originates. It might take a little while, but keep practising until you get all these sensations in place. Then repeat it for as many times as you need to, in order to be able to switch into that mode of perception in an instant or two at most.

This, ladies and gents, is you sensing the core of the energy body (Hamr) and from it the first and most intense energetic radiation outward. As you progress, keep expanding how far out you can feel the pulse flow. For some, it will not be too far, while for others, it will be much further out. The average human being has a three-foot radiation, at which point you hit the inner 'skin' or 'shell' of your spherical shape. With a little dedication you should be able to extend this practice to the point where you find yourself walking down the street feeling the energy body (Hamr) core directing the physical movement AND feeling its full spherical/egg shape moving. Eventually, you can perceive yourself as a sphere of energy moving forward when walking down the street.

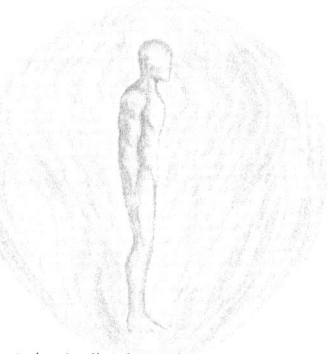
Spherically shaped energy body

Egg shaped energy body

When doing this, it is important to not only focus on the front of the body – far too much of our awareness is directed forward, so make sure you focus on being able to do this through the back as well and the sides, and above and below. Remember, the energy body (Hamr) is spherical, so you will find it in all directions! Becoming skilled in this is essential before moving onto any other practice. At this stage, you are establishing the foundation of energy body (Hamr) perception which in turn leads you to control.

With a little dedication, you should be able to extend this practice to the point where you find yourself walking down the street, feeling the energy body (Hamr) core directing the physical movement, AND feeling its full spherical shape moving. Eventually, you can perceive yourself as a sphere of energy moving forward when walking down the street with little to no effort.

Quick Steps

1 Start by sitting in a chair with legs together and arms on the legs (quads). Remain still and breathe, relaxing, allowing all tension to dissipate.
2 Focus on your body, on its physicality and how solid it feels.
3 You should notice the slight pulse of energy on your skin (providing you have remained perfectly still). Enjoy its dance and motion on and through your skin's surface.
4 Concentrate that YOU, and your very presence and persona, are on the inside of your skin. If it helps, you can imagine it as how a layer of clothing would feel. It is from the YOU

inside the skin that this energy pulse originates, pulsing outwards.

5 Repeat these initial steps until you no longer need to put additional effort to trigger the perception(s).

6 As you keep doing this, try to expand how far you can feel this outwards energy pulsing. Typical human beings will have a total pulsating radiation of about three feet. At that point, you will sense the Inside Boundary of your sphere. Remember, your sense of Self is the inner part within your body. The Inner Boundary of your spherical energy body shape is what you can think of as the most distant point of your auric field. This makes perfect sense, if you keep in mind that what mankind calls the aura is in fact the largest part of the energy body itself.

7 Repeat as many times as necessary until this awareness of your entire energy body (Hamr) becomes a reflex you can turn on within an instant or two. It is important to do this sensing in a spherical manner, not just focusing on the front of your body or its left or right. Your energy body (Hamr) is ALL around your physical, in ALL directions (including above and below).

8 When you have mastered this, as you walk in the street, turn on this sensory perception of the energy body (Hamr) in your daily activities. But remember not to allow it to distract you from the physical environment! There is nothing worse than being focussed on it and getting into harm's way because you are ignoring the things around you in

the process. This awareness needs to flow SIMULTANEOUSLY to the physical AND you need to have a perfect distinction between the physical and energetic. It is only this way that you can stretch awareness, rather than just shift it to one or the other.

Once you have reached this stage, also focus on the fact that when you get close to other people, your energy sphere overlaps with theirs (they blend into each other). Or if you are strong enough, you can harden the outer layers of your sphere in order to push other energies away around you. Getting to that point simply requires you to focus in on the outer skin of the energy body (Hamr) and intend it to become more solid, to disallow any other energy in. Any energy which hits against such a hardened outer layer will simply flow around its 'shell'. Naturally, there is no need to push your skills to this point for the practices in this book (but it will definitely do you no harm to do so, if you feel like perfecting them!). Remember what we discussed when talking about having fun with respect to the biological awareness. Time to have fun with this!

Biologically Aware Hamr

Ah, the gold standard of energy body potential activation! Many traditions have their students spend an entire lifetime in meditation trying to achieve this. This is not so for the Norse mystic. We have a very simple and quick practice in order to achieve the same end results with a few added bonuses to go!

Start by doing exactly the same as in the practice given above. Once you have reached the point where you can sense the whole of your energy body (including the whole sphere or auric field, if you prefer), feel the inside of the outer shell/skin. Anchor your perception until it is nice and firm. When you no longer need to consciously focus on it much but still have full awareness of it, you are ready for the next step.

This involves becoming aware of your biological awareness. Since this has been dealt with at length in the previous sections' practices, it should present no problem whatsoever. The trick is to start expanding this awareness, or rather extending it (if you prefer, you can think of it as stretching as well). Keep on doing so until it is flowing through the skin and into the energy body(Hamr)'s sphere. Keep on expanding until at long last you manage to expand it all throughout the entire sphere, up to the inner wall of its shell. This will be hard and a gradual process – there is no point beating around the bush about it. It will take time, and it may sometimes feel like you are not making much progress. Keep at it, as developing the ability to do this and finally maintaining your biological awareness throughout the entire energy body (Hamr) is absolutely essential. It is one of the reasons for which the Self is structured in the manner it is (well, these parts of it, in any case).

Once you have achieved this extension of biological awareness through the sphere of the energy body (Hamr), the next step is to expand it back inwards to the core. Remember, in the practice you just learnt, you expand it from the physical outwards, so the part of the energy body (Hamr) which is the core and is within the physical (Lik) has not been subject to the influences of the biological awareness – not yet. Your goal is to expose the whole energy body (Hamr) to it, and over the course of time, teach it not only to host that awareness but to teach the biological awareness to inhabit the energy body (Hamr). In other words, to stretch and blend the one into the other. Once you have fully unlocked this skill, you will be able to start taking direct control of the energy body (Hamr) by blending your consciousness into the mix. Blending the Spirit (Óðr) into the biological awareness has been covered in the previous section. Back to our current task at hand.

Start as you did in the previous practice until you reach the point where your biological awareness is nice and stable, expanded throughout the energy body

(Hamr)'s sphere. Maintain it this way and will it to expand inwards now, right through the skin of the physical body (Lik), back into it but not into the flesh itself. Rather, expand it inwards through the skin and into the energy body (Hamr)'s core (remember that layer on the inside of the physical?). Once there, expand it throughout the whole of the energy body (Hamr) core. Once you have achieved this, feel its activation or presence in both the inside and the outside of the core.

Quick Steps

1   Start by establishing your awareness of the energy body (Hamr) as you did in the practice above. When you feel the outer shell of the energy body's surface without having to maintain focus on it, you may proceed.
2   Next, become aware of your biological awareness as you have done in the Section 2 practices. It should be almost a reflex by now to do so, and should present no issues. What you are going to do is to start expanding (or stretching) this awareness from each and every cell of your physical body (Lik) outwards. Avoid thinking of it as a detaching process – this will damage your cell's functions – instead intend it to grow and stretch, whilst still anchored in the very cells it originates from.
3   Each time you practice this, increase this stretch/expansion by a tiny amount (an absolute maximum of half an inch, and never more!). You are teaching your biology something which takes time (a lot of time, for that

matter). Go slow and steady, better than breaking something. Keep on repeating until you have grown it to include the whole energy body (Hamr) up to the outermost shell/skin of its spherical shape. That means also the auric field, if you prefer to think of it that way.

4. Having reached this first goal, it is time to expand inwards! Up to this point, you were growing your biological awareness out of the physical into the outer part of the energy body (Hamr). Once that is nice and stable, expand it back inwards so that it floods the core of the energy body (Hamr), which is inside the physical body (Lik). The simplest way to do this is to focus on the biological awareness you have already stretched, and intend it to start 'stretching' further, but inwards. Think of it as expanding to fill the entire sphere of your energy body (Hamr). Since it has already grown outwards, it can only grow inwards now. This will layer the biology with the core of the energy body AND the physical body (since the two parts overlap). Once again, expand it slowly, a step at a time, but this time, you need to make sure you DO NOT lose it from the outer parts.

5. At this stage, you should be able to feel it in each and every nook and cranny of the energy body (Hamr).

6. Rinse and repeat until this is achieved as a reflex, without much need to focus on any part of the practice.

At this point, you should have biological awareness flowing and present in each and every part of the energy body (Hamr). Every nook and cranny should be permeated by it. Spend some time acclimatising yourself to this until you can keep it pulsating in the energy body (Hamr) at will. Once again, be patient and persistent. Mastering this to as close to perfection as possible is essential and one of the great keys to personal evolution.

Once you have achieved a reasonable level of mastery at expanding and blending your biological awareness through the energy body (Hamr), start working on blending the Spirit (Óðr) into the biological awareness, before you expand it throughout the energy body (the entire sphere of it). This is a nice additional boost you can do, even at this stage of development of the Self.

This is then typically extended throughout the energy body organs, otherwise known as Hvels (to the Norse or proto-Europeans) or Chakras (for those of Eastern tradition mind-sets), but seeing as it is not necessary at this point and there is limited space, we will deal with them at a later point in time and give them the space and detail they deserve.

You should be aware that as you work through this, you will start to awaken the energy body (Hamr). Make sure you keep the flow of Megin (by increasing the Hamingja work)[56] as it will require more and more power to maintain that activation. On the upside, even though it is more work, you will gain many benefits, including developing the ability to become aware within it. This will signal your awakening, and non-physical forms of consciousness will start to notice you and try to entice you. Always remember that Midgard and your physical body (Lik) are your home, and do not get tricked into agreeing to stay anywhere else (for the time being, in any case). Keep your Self as the master of your progression, not some other 'thing' out there. Many will tempt you, and they simply cannot resist. Should things get too intense, pull your biological awareness back into the core of the energy body (Hamr) and avoid expanding it into the rest of its spherical shape. At least, for a little while. When you have had a break, return to full expansion. The same runs true of not inviting or allowing those non-physical forms of awareness into yourself or Midgard! Using the ᛉ Óðal (Othala), ᚢ Úr (Uruz) and ᛗ Maður (Mannaz) runes can help solidify your Self against their bothersome intrusions or the ᛉ Ýr (Elhaz), and ᚦ Þurs (Thurisaz) runes can help with protection from them. The ᛏ Týr (Tiwaz) and ᛜ Ing (Ingwaz) runic energies are excellent when it comes to making your energy body (Hamr) an inhospitable place for them to attach to or communicate with.

Seeing The Energy of The Energy Body Sphere

This one is a fun practice! Sit still as you did when doing the 'Perception of the Energy Body' but this time, make sure you are facing a blank wall. As long as it is not painted with too dark a colour, it will work just fine. Once you have achieved the stillness and can feel the energy radiate on the surface of your skin, look straight ahead but focus on the immediate space in front of you, rather than on the wall itself. If you can manage it, sense your sight coming into the physical eye from the energy body (Hamr)'s eyes (remember, its core is shaped like the physical – hence all the organ shapes are, superimposed on each other). If you retain your focus on seeing from the energy body (Hamr) eyes through the physical (Lik) and look at the space in front of you, intend to see the energy there.

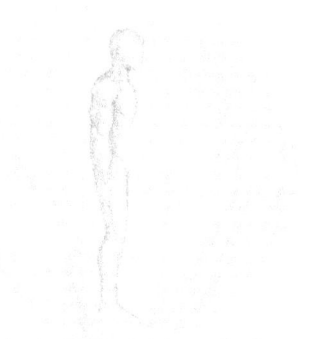
Spherically shaped energy body

You are, in effect, trying to see those parts of the energy body (Hamr) which are typically called the aura from inside the energy body (Hamr).

With a bit of practice, you will at first be able to see tiny sparkle-like particles, very much as an energetic type of dust, erratically floating about in all directions. Then, with a little extra practice, you will be able to notice thin waves of energy flowing through those. More than this one cannot put into words, because it will depend entirely on each individual and how your energy body (Hamr) flows. Even with the two things just mentioned (the sparks and flow), these might not be present or be different. It is important for all these practices to make your own observations. Use these just as a guide for what to look out for, but if what you see does not match, that is fine – it will most probably not match. The important thing is that you are seeing something! Always remember, individual differences are a vital key!

Connecting with
The Energy Body (Hamr)

Making that connection with the energy body (Hamr) is of critical importance but is also one of the most difficult things we have to do. The first steps always are, are they not? Connecting with the energy body (Hamr) is a mammoth task, not due to complexity or intricacy of the practices (those are actually mind-numbingly simple), but in terms of achievement. You will need a lot of spare energy to make this connection, and here we are not talking about feeling good and refreshed – the energy involved is the energy of awareness and that is very limited for human beings, especially in today's day and age. Even a slight lack of energy and you will be hard pushed, if at all able, to make this connection. Making it is the first step in maintaining it, and developing the ability to re-establish it at will is even more tricky. So why bother? Because it is only by doing so that we can awaken it, and to do that enables it to become a vehicle for our conscious awareness. Being able to shift our primary seat of consciousness from the physical into the energetic is a vital step for both evolution and survival, after death of the physiology. It is only in our energy bodies (Hamr) that we can gain the ability to express our true selves, beyond the constraints imposed upon such expression of Self by physical limitation.

So how do we gain the required energy reserves? If you have been working through *The Spirit of Húnir Awakens*, you will have learnt to limit the unnecessary waste incurred via behaviours, social norms, language, thought and so forth. Having worked through *The Breath of Oðin Awakens*, you will have learnt how to amplify the amount of Megin stored in the Hamingja and circulate it via DNA into the body (Lik) and then subsequently into the energy body (Hamr). Finally, in this book, you will have learnt how, by observing the sanctity of the body and not injuring it, not losing blood and not exposing it to certain energy wastage activities, how to enhance its physicality and thereby energetic gravity, which all contribute to greater energy reserves. Skipping to the chapters dealing with the Shadow body (Sal), you will learn how to add energy from the 'dark matter' regions to your Being, thereby adding an additional layer for use in awakening the energy body (Hamr). Being persistent with all these practices, they will yield sufficient energy to propel you forward. When you come to using actual High Galdr, you will learn to add those runic currents to your energy sources as well.

For the time being, practice what you have learnt so far and to those practices, add the ones given below. It is impossible to know exactly when you have sufficient energetic resources for this other than by practising it until it all falls into place (otherwise referred to as 'all clicking into place'). This is due to the fact that each individual will have different energy requirements, with some energy body (Hamr) awakening very rapidly with little effort, whilst others seeming to require a climb up Mount Everest! Do not despair if it takes you a long time. The more powerful the energy body (Hamr) and the more scope it has, the more difficult it is to awaken. Once it does, it also takes more energy to maintain and nourish than a quickly awakening one with more limited scope. In any case, as you as you start to see energy, you are on the right track. If you are able to see non-physical beings, you are already awake and just need to nourish it more. Those who as children have developed these skills and have maintained them throughout their lives have fast-awakening energy bodies.

Establishing The Connection

This is a very simple practice. Start off by spending a few minutes relaxing and allowing your mind to clear out all the daily nonsense it is usually preoccupied with. Just think 'relax' and take a few deep breaths to let go of the world around you. You will feel tension flooding out of your body of its own accord. There is no need for any complex tighten-loosen practices – those just cause disturbances in the entire process. Close your eyes and relax. Simple, effective. This will place you in a mild relaxed-trance state. That is all you need here.

The actual step involved is only one. Intend to connect with the energy body (Hamr), harmonise and become one with it. If you like, you can also intend to perceive from WITHIN it. That is all you need to do. Naturally, this requires mastery of intent, but seeing as we have covered that, you should at least have some basic skill in it. All you do here is intend and unleash that intent over and over and over again. Providing the energy is there, you will at first find yourself either in the energy body (Hamr) itself or you will perceive from within it. The first few times, it is only a very short shift, hence a limited experience, but it is profound no matter how long it lasts. The more often you do this and the more energy you build up, the longer it will last and the sharper it will become, until you are building the required 'connections' and with each attempt, you are pushing forward. Eventually, if you persist at it, that proverbial wall will crack and break!

Gender Advantages

Because of our physiological differences and due to the fact that each organ within our body has not only a biological function but also an energetic one, we all have certain strengths (and weaknesses) when it comes to this type of work.

Men have the ability to enhance their intent via the secondary functions of their testicles. Women have an incredibly enhanced perceptive advantage when it comes to energy perception in general, by using the secondary function of their vagina. We will look at these in detail when it comes to dealing with sexual Seiðr practices. For the time being, the best way to make use of these is to 'switch them on' before doing the practice given above.

How you do so is just as inherently simple. Perform the same relaxation as outlined above, then focus on the organ(s) in question (for men, BOTH the testicles and for women, the whole of the vagina). You need to feel them, then simply intend them to increase the power and scope of your intent (for men) or to awaken full perception of the energy level of reality (for women). Go slow with these, as they can cause large changes in your energy system (for both the physical and the energy body (Hamr)).

If you are missing these organs, unfortunately, there is nothing you can do about it and the only course of action is to skip this altogether. Some will argue that even after having the organ removed it is still in the blueprint (the energy body). That is correct, but what is in the blueprint is exactly that: the blueprint for generating the organ, NOT the organ itself. What we are using here is the energetic function of the PHYSICAL organs. The sexual organs and their correct functioning are very important when working with the energy body (Hamr), the shadow body (Sal) and the physical body (Lik). There is simply no escaping that.

If in doubt, skip this practice and do the main one given above. It will take longer but will not stop you from achieving your goal.

- The Blood of Lóðurr Awakens -

THE SHADOW SELF (SAL)

Introducing the Shadow Self (Sal)

The shadow (Sal) is one of the most mysterious parts of the energetic Self, seldom ever discussed, and often simply understood in terms of what people think a shadow version of the Self would be like. Unlike what you would typically understand as a shadow in terms of standard human psychology, the shadow (Sal) is completely different to our modern-day understanding of the concept.

It is probably the most misunderstood of all parts of the Self. This part of the Self was highly developed in terms of Seiðr practices and other than in the Berserker warriors who used Seiðr trances, it was seldom if ever mentioned. Hence, traditionally speaking, it was not spoken of, nor was knowledge of it shared with 'outsiders' and even more so, it was seldom ever written about.

Times change and it is now time to shed some light on this all-too-hidden part of the Self. The Sal always refers to the shadow Self (or shadow body). However, what the 'shadow' word meant was an entire mystery in its own right.

The modern-day concept of a shadow part of the Self is mainly defined in terms of psychology – or, more accurately, psychotherapies – which have bled over into new age practices. In that context, the shadow is seen as a part of the Self which holds all the things and characteristics of the Self which are rejected by the conscious or which the current conscious self cannot express.

Regardless, we are interested in actual knowledge linked to the shadow (Sal) in Norse terms. For us, it is one of the nine parts of the Self and hence an essential component of our totality of Being. As you can see from (the illustration below) it sits at the bottom of the energetic level of the Self. Interestingly, it also sits in direct opposition to the energy body (Hamr).

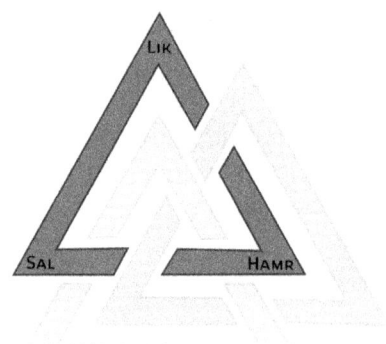

The shadow (Sal) located at the bottom left

What The Sal is NOT

Modern understanding of what the 'shadow Self' could be is typically fuelled by what one could term psychology mixed up with new age nonsense. Such theories are centred around the concept of the shadow including all the things you consciously exclude or reject.

Why this is nonsensical is simple: such theories revolve around the possibility of us including everything, which in evolutionarily terms, is a null point. The reasoning behind this is that if an ultimate being incarnates by limiting him or herself into a form, all that which is 'locked away' is then contained in the shadow Self. This theory fails because it makes evolution totally pointless: ancestral transmission of experiences and memory, increases of power, growth of consciousness, expansion of perception and so forth would all be totally meaningless. It would also make the shadow so overwhelmingly powerful that it would simply be impossible to control and would run amok willy-nilly, due to the fact that it can overpower you whenever and however it wants. As such, it gains a very illogical and odd connotation where the shadow, according to that definition, would in theory contain absolute power, knowledge, awareness and everything else because none of those are expressed by the conscious. In other words, it would make actual evolution totally pointless and all that would ever be needed would be the integration of all the shadow contains into the conscious, at which point this shadow Self would cease to exist. With all due respect to those pushing and believing this view, it is totally nonsensical. Any sensible thinking on this theory will result in the conclusion that it is unrealistic and entirely flawed.

With that out of the way, let us look at what our ancestors referred to as the Sal (shadow). As expected, very much as they were, it is practical and down to earth.

Understanding The Sal

The shadow (Sal) is described as the shadow not due to it being a shadow per se, although it has strong similarities to it. Simply put, the Sal is the 'emptiness' found in between the energy body (Hamr) and the inner physical layer of the skin. Scientifically speaking, it has been established that matter is actually particles separated by large amounts of space. The same happens with our bodies and energy bodies. The shadow (Sal) is found in that emptiness, in the space in between the energy body (Hamr) and the physical (Lik).

The shadow (Sal) is not the emptiness; it is found in what you perceive as being emptiness. This might seem confusing but it is very simple, once approached practically. As you can imagine, there is no actual emptiness in our bodies, since that is an anti-creation part of the Gap and is not found within creation itself. The reason why that space in between particles is usually perceived as empty is that human perception does not allow for the type of perception needed to directly see, feel and experience the shadow (Sal) or its level of being. In order to do so, you need the perceptions of the shadow (Sal) itself. This raises a catch twenty-two situation, where

The Shadow body (Sal) emanating from within

the shadow (Sal) cannot be perceived without the shadow (Sal)'s abilities and reaching it requires those perceptual abilities. A bit of a problem. This is the main reason why gaining awareness of the energy body (Hamr) was key, prior to starting working with the shadow (Sal), as you will need to use it to gain access to the shadow (Sal). More on this below. The reason it was referred to as 'shadow' was simply that the energetic light of the energy body (Hamr) reflects and the inner gaps/emptiness within us are perceived as something which reflects back, which is shadow substance! This is what shadow energy actually is – born out of a cast-off reflection of light.

Functions of The Sal

The shadow (Sal) is an important part of the Self. It is the link with the unseen, with what in modern-day scientific terminology is called the dark side of our universe. Dark matter is its substance and dark matter combined with dark energy fuels it. The Sal, in effect, holds the totality of the energetic matter (which is pure substance with dark energy) of this level of the Self.

The concept of energy and matter being one is very much prevalent these days. However, they are not quite one and the same. Matter can be thought of as consolidated energy, energy which has gone through all five phases of manifestation until it has become matter. The issue of matter vs energy is a complex one – for now, suffice it to say that there is infinite matter in Creation as a whole. The issue is that the human mind, in its current state, thinks of things only in terms of the current physical level it is in. In other words, when told that there is infinite matter or that the shadow

(Sal) is matter, people immediately think, "Of course not. It cannot be seen and science says matter is finite." Well, that would be true, if matter was only physical at that level of physicality which can be perceived by the average human mind – and hence also by human sciences, for only that which the human mind can sense or perceive can be included in sciences invented by mankind. They are, after all, products of the human mind. However, this is far from the case. There are many types of matter, at many levels of density, some observable by scientific instruments and others not. What is termed dark matter is another type of matter, although a critically important one. It is known that dark matter does not interact electromagnetically with our current mode of perceived reality. Instead, it does so through gravity. In Old Norse terms, it interacts and impacts the Ice principle which, if you think about it, makes perfect sense since the original principle of darkness comes forth from Niflheim. This important interaction will be covered in a lot more detail later on. For now, it is very important to keep in mind that this is a dominant principle in our reality, accounting for 84.5% of the total mass of our universe.[57] Modern-day cosmic theories account for the formation of galaxies and their evolution streaming from dark matter.

    This fits perfectly with the Norse teachings of the Self. At the energetic level, the energy body (Hamr) is energy and vibrant light, the shadow (Sal) is dark matter and substance and the physical (Lik) is the root/product of both. How well this matches with the universal theories of dark and physical matter is most fascinating. These theoretical and practical synchronicities will keep popping up for those who pay close attention and are a fundamental way of 'rubber stamping' their validity.

Sal - The Dark Side of our Self

We are both light and dark. There is no denying the fact that each and every human being has both compassion and darkness within themselves. After all, in this dualistic reality, both are needed for anything and everything to exist. If the one is lacking, the other cannot be. This seems like a fundamentally challenging concept for practically all traditions to deal with. Most will ignore one in exclusive preference of the other, whilst others will simply try to suppress one in favour of the other. Either of these approaches causes substantial conflict within the Self. We have already seen that ignoring or suppressing any of the various aspects of the Self leads to loss of balance and harmony within, as well as the possibility of the suppressed part causing no end of trouble.

In the Norse tradition, the Völva and Seiðr crafts were very much focused on the use, development and mastery of the shadow (Sal), whereas Galdr was more concerned with the energy body (Hamr). However, both are interrelated and hence need to be mastered in order to allow the full breadth of potential within us to be unleashed. Rather than seek to suppress the shadow (Sal) in favour of the energy body (Hamr), we are going to take the approach of the Wise Norse Women and learn to master it, or at least understand it. Understanding our own darkness is half the battle of understanding our Self since it belongs to the energetic side of reality, just as the energy body (Hamr) and physical (Lik) do. It is important to do so.

We will go a step further and walk the path of Woden in this task, merging the shadow (Sal) and the energy body (Hamr) along with the physical body (Lik)'s biological awareness, which is the first essential foundation needed for preserving the Self after death.

It is worth remembering that you will first have to have connected with the energy body (Hamr) and the light and fire runes. The fundamental rule is: first you master the light, then you can safely work with the dark. Doing it in any other way will put you at risk of losing your Self to the dark or be drowned/deceived by it. Even if you keep watch for this risk and do your best to avoid it, you will never be able to fully master the dark without having done so with the light first. This will be a highly controversial statement for all those interested in the so-called dark ways but the wise among you will understand perfectly why this is so.

For those who refuse to listen to the advice given, you have been warned. What you do with this is entirely up to you. You will have no one to blame but yourself. For those who have gained a solid foothold in the 'light' side of things, no matter what their experiences with the dark, they will never be sunk and lost in it, irrespective of how overpowering or consuming it gets. There are no but ifs, no buts, no exceptions, no "I'm specials" to this universal principle. It is like all other principles of Creation: unyielding and unbending. Without the power of Light, there is no mastery of the Dark, no matter how much one deludes oneself otherwise.

Connecting with The Sal

This is the easiest part of the Self to connect with and at the same time, the most difficult. In order to do so, you will have to have mastered the 'Becoming Conscious of the Óðr (Spirit)' practice[58] pretty much perfectly. As you shift into the Spirit (Óðr), then become aware of it being within the energy body (Hamr). Focus in on the energy body (Hamr). Here, you should notice that unlike the Spirit (Óðr), it is not free flowing but has cohesion and a type of 'togetherness' which yields boundaries and hence shape. Concentrate on its outer shape and notice how it sits within the boundary of the physical (Lik).

Pay close attention here. Since the energy body (Hamr) and the physical (Lik) have shape and boundary, you should be able to notice the most minute gaps in between them. You might have to try to zoom into them over several attempts but with firm conviction, you will succeed in noticing them. As you notice the first, pay attention to the one next to it and so forth, until eventually, you have a view of all these micro-energetic gaps in between the energy body's (Hamr) boundary and the Inner Boundary of the physical body (Lik). This is where you find your shadow (Sal) – well, its core in any case.

Once you have managed to get good at noticing them and can not only do so with ease but also maintain awareness of them all without strain or effort, you are ready to proceed. As you keep awareness flowing of all these in-between gaps, will, or better yet, intend your shadow (Sal) to pour out of them. With the shadow (Sal) it is fluid – it has no hard shape or form but is rather like a very dense shadow with substance (a type of thickness). As you keep the intent flowing, you will notice it spilling out from all these micro-gaps until it fills all the space in between the energy body (Hamr) and physical body (Lik). Keep the intent going and the shadow (Sal) flowing outwards until you reach the point where it is like a thick smoky substance dancing all over you. The shadow on the inner part of you needs to be spilling outwards to about one to three inches from your skin.

Enjoy it, feel it, know it. If you are a male, use your will to force it into submission. It is the only feminine part of the Self upon which we impose forcefully. The stronger your will the better. Learn to rule it with an iron grip, if need be. If you are a female mystic, manipulate it and coax it into following your conscious direction. It is a very different way of working with the shadow (Sal), depending on your gender. This is unavoidable because the shadow (Sal) of a male and a female is very different, even if they are both manifestations of the 'same' part of the Self. Men will feel it as cool and having a bit of static flowing through it, while women will feel it as a soft coldness. This, of course, is according to biological gender. If our modern-day understanding of gender no longer matches the energy realities, as with all other things, energy will override all the human perceptions and understandings of things as an overarching principle.

Quick Steps

1. Shift into the Spirit (Óðr), then become aware of being within the energy body (Hamr). Focus in on the energy body. Notice how it now has a certain level of cohesion (if it does not, you should perform the previous practices in the energy body (Hamr) section further).
2. Concentrate on the 'outer' layer of the core of your energy body (remember, the part of it within the physical, under the skin).
3. Settle down into that perception and pay close attention to how this energy body (Hamr) core sits within the physical, wearing the latter as an additional skin or a suit of clothing. If you pay close attention, you will eventually notice that there is a tiny gap in between the inner surface of the physical body (Lik)'s skin and the outer layer of the core of your energy body (Hamr). There are hundreds of thousands of minute gaps between the two. It might take a few attempts to notice them. If you have trouble, use intent to stretch your perceptive skills to pick them up.
4. When you have gained the ability to notice

them effortlessly, congratulations, you have found the entry points for the shadow (Sal). Keep on working at it until you can hold onto the perception of ALL those gaps simultaneously. It is hard, damn hard, but it is the only way to expand your perceptive abilities to bridge them into shadow perceptions.

5   Intend your shadow (Sal) to pour out of those gaps. It will seem like a dense shadowy substance with a type of thickness. Keep the intent flowing and the substance will flow. It will fill all those gaps in between the energy body (Hamr) and physical body (Lik). Keep it flowing until it gathers about one to three inches all over your physical skin.

6   Keep it bound to your physical skin by willing it to remain so. All men do so by forcing it to do so – aggressive will is the only way a male can control his shadow. Women do so by coaxing it and manipulating it to comply with her will. It is the only way the shadow of a woman will respond.

7   Men should feel this substance as cool with a bit of a static flow through it every so often, women feel theirs as soft coolness. Do note all these gender distinctions work in accordance with the energetic gender dynamics. It is an unchangeable principle of Creation.

# Using The Sal and Gaining Control

As mentioned above, the manner in which men and women do so is very different. Keep that in mind and use the appropriate method depending on your (biological) gender. Avoid being 'creative' in anything you do with the shadow (Sal) part of your Self. Not because being creative is bad – quite to the contrary – but not when working with this part of the Self because it is ultimately exceedingly more creative than you will ever be capable of being. It is capable of taking any creative experimenting and twisting it to its own uses, in order to trap you into a situation where it is in control and not you. Even a slight hint of loss of control should be immediate instant cause for stopping the practice. If it ever takes over, it will devour your entire Self. This is the part of the Self which slips in between the other parts and slips into parts you might not even be aware of yet. Be cautious and remain in control.

This is also one of the key reasons we leave it so late in our explorations of the Self. Not only are you dealing with the difficulties mentioned, but you are also dealing with the part of the Self which is the store and source of all dark matter within you. In other words, it has vast amounts of fuel to work with. One of the advantages we gain by mastering the shadow (Sal) is the use of that substance which bridges things into the state of matter. It is, if you prefer, where energy and matter mix and cross over into each other. This is why all beings in existence have a shadow (Sal).

Back to the practice: follow the steps you did in connecting with the shadow (Sal) as outlined above, until you get to the point where you have your shadow (Sal) spilt out and dancing all over your skin, thickening there. When you are at this stage, shift back into the Spirit (Óðr) and from within it, expand into the shadow (Sal). What you are doing is spilling the flow of Spirit (Óðr) into your shadow (Sal) and intermixing them. Your shadow (Sal) will change slightly to gain a slight hue, which represents the brilliance of awareness now flowing through it. At this point, you can start gaining control of it using the gender-based methodology given above. As you do, meditate on being the shadow (Sal) Self. Since it is flowing through and around your physical body (Lik), this should be a relatively simple thing to do. The point you want to get to is where you are aware only of being flowing shadowy matter and forget about your physical body (Lik) completely.

You will feel the dark side of your Self whilst within the shadow (Sal). Remember to keep control – whatever negative impulses or feelings crop up, they all need to be acknowledged and released. Avoid at all costs holding onto those whilst merged with your shadow Self (Sal). This is the path to sinking and losing yourself in the dark. If you allow it to trigger you in this way, it becomes the seat of control at the expense of your conscious awareness. You do not want to subject yourself to the same fate Loki had when he lost control of himself and was consumed by his own shadow (Sal).

To end the practice, pull back all the shadow into your physical body (Lik) and then pull the Spirit (Óðr) out of it and back to its original place. Note, we are not pulling the shadow (Sal) back into the gaps from where it originated. We want it to remain dancing in between the energy body (Hamr)'s Outer and physical body (Lik)'s Inner Borders. This is what brings it into the scope of awareness, which is exactly where we need and want it to be.

Quick Steps

1. Follow the steps for the practice above until you get to the point where you have your shadow (Sal) spilt out and dancing all over your body's skin, thickening there.
2. Shift back to your Spirit (Óðr). From within it, expand throughout the shadow (Sal) you have just exteriorised around your physical. This mixes Spirit (Óðr) and shadow (Sal), resulting in many advantages. You should notice a certain level of brilliance or reflectiveness in the shadow sub-

Fully Formed Shadow Self (Sal)

stance now, for as long as you maintain that mix.
3 Using the gender-based methods, you will have to establish control of it. Men: wilful dominance, women: compliant manipulation are the keys to work with. The more control you establish, the more you will lose focus of the physical body (Lik), the energy body (Hamr) and all things around you, and the more you will shift your focus and awareness into the shadow (Sal).
4 Rinse and repeat until you are only aware of being the shadow (Sal) and nothing else.
5 Doing this, you will feel the dark within you. All the negative characteristics of your personality, all the dark desires and tendencies will start to surface in your mind. You need to face these head on and never allow them to take over. If you do, the shadow Self (Sal) will consume your awareness and eventually the whole of you. In those cases, you will have lost control and it will cost you more dearly than you can ever imagine. Proceed cautiously, and limit your time with these practices! Better to establish control a few minutes a day than attempt an hour and fall prey to it. You have been warned.
6 End by pulling the shadow substance back into the physical and then pulling the Spirit (Óðr) back to its original place, if you have trouble doing so, just pull it back into the physical brain and it will automatically relocate. Note, you are not pulling the shadow substance back into the gaps. Instead, you

leave it flowing in between the physical (Lik) and energy bodies (Hamr).

Notes on Advanced Shadow (Sal) Work

There is a vast body of knowledge available for the rune mystic in respect of the shadow (Sal), its usage and methods to amplify it. Due to their complexity and dangers, we are just touching upon the very basics required for Galdr work. Some of the other secrets of the shadow (Sal) might be covered at a later time in Seiðr work and in a lot more depth when dealing with Shadow Galdr. For the time being, the potential for harm when working with this part of the Self is rather high and requires you to be fully prepared with mastery of High Galdr to safely undertake even the intermediary practices in this area of the Self.

- The Blood of Lóðurr Awakens -

Triangular Relationship: Physical (Lik) – Shadow (Sal) Energy (Hamr)

A few notes are worthwhile on this topic before we move on. Most will assume that this is all energetic and think it has no effect(s) on the physical body (Lik). This is a misconception. For one thing, ultimately speaking, everything is first and foremost energy and secondly, matter. Because the shadow Self (Sal) sits in between the energetic and matter, its affects are on both. Naturally, polarity is in play here where this pole and anti-pole interact across other dualities and polarities. This gets a little complex when trying to put it into words but let us have a go at it nonetheless.

For men: their physical polarity is the primary one (in other words, active), and the energy body (Hamr) is the secondary (in other words, passive). The shadow (Sal) sits between these and acts on both because it is neither a neural nor dual polarity but neither, and hence is affecting both. Because male shadows are female in their base nature, they are passive. This is why perception of energy realms is so damn hard for men to develop – they have a dual negative passivity (on the shadow (Sal) and on the energy body (Hamr)). This is also why men are so focused on the physical and mental (they have a positive or active polarity on both these levels).

When men develop their shadows and introduce fire rune influences into them (which are activating and masculinising in terms of polarities), the enhancement of the shadow will enhance their physical bodies (Lik) first and foremost. The added density in men will reflect in the gradual increase in muscle fibre density. So, if you are a (biological) male and are not actively working out with the goal to build muscle, GO DO IT NOW. The benefits of your energy work will be dulled down otherwise, because you are not in possession of a feedback loop. What is this loop? It plays on the laws of polarity: where the active polarity on the shadow (Sal) is enhanced, it feeds back to the active polarity on the physical body (Lik). When the active polarity on the physical is enhanced, it feeds back to the active polarity on the shadow. The more this looping of energy and matter circulates, the more effective and powerful it becomes on both bodies or parts of the Self. Once this polarity loop is at maximum potential, it has no other place to expand in than the energy body (Hamr). In those cases, it starts to activate the energy body (Hamr) and ALL its perceptive abilities, as well as our ability to consciously control it. Eventually, the energy body (Hamr) is pushed from a state of passive negativity to one of activity.

For women: their physical bodies are negative in polarity, and this gives rise to attraction. They draw your attention to them, you experience a pull on your focus, similar to a type of gravitational pull on the mind. However, their energy bodies (Hamr) are of the active pole and so is their shadow (Sal) – the (biological) female has a masculine shadow Self (Sal). This is why they are so perceptive of energy: both bodies which deal with energy are on the opposite pole (are active). Yet their perception cannot gain depth or persistence until the physical awareness is brought into play. When they work on their shadow Self (Sal) and turn it negative, the feedback loop is triggered with the physical. The same runs true as with men: the more powerful the shadow, the more powerful the physical. Here, we do not see an increase in density of muscle or its fibres. Instead, we see an increase in fluidity and flow of energy through the physical. Reshaping the physical becomes easy, because attractiveness or charisma is another facet of this fluidity that is greatly increased – as is the capacity to adapt. The more these energies grow on the physical, the more they give feedback to the shadow, which in turn loops back. It is not something you gain from artificially 'enhancing' the physical, it is something you gain by harmonious feedback in between the shadow and the physical. Once that loop is at its maximum potential, it expands into the energy body (Hamr) just as it does with men. However, for women, it does not activate it (since their energy bodies are already active in some shape or form). Instead, it gives it cohesion and solidity of shape, allowing it to maintain and become a vehicle for consciousness. The difference in gender here is something purely on the order of these things awakening and the order in which it is done. Men have the cohesion (or gain it very easily) while women need to work on it, but women, on the other hand, have perception and easy activation of the energy body (Hamr) whereas men need to work hard on theirs. For both genders, once the two are gained (cohesion/solidity of shape AND activation), you can use them as an independent vehicle for perception, awareness and consciousness of energy realities.

This, ladies and gents, completes the preparatory learning and training for High Galdr. Having learnt to make flow your Breath (Önd), to generate and store Megin with the Hamingja, to work directly from within your Spirit (Óðr), to send the ravens of mind (Hugr) and memory (Minni) out, to use your physical bodies (Lik) by unleashing biological awareness, to master your blood and DNA's hidden potentials, to awaken your energy body (Hamr), to start working with your shadow (Sal) and to unleash your Intent, you are now well prepared to undertake the first steps in learning and mastering actual Galdr, which is called 'High Galdr' or 'Galdr of the High'.

It also completes mastery of all but one part of the Self. Integration of the entire Self should be well underway for all those who have diligently practised so far. Awareness, perceptions and consciousness will have expanded to a significant degree. The Fylgja will be covered after High Galdr, and upon integrating that final part of the Self, you will have achieved something incredible: the birth of a unique Being in the eyes of Creation. One ready to stand on his or her own in Creation. Then, you will be finally able to utter 'I AM' to all of existence.

Next stop: actual High Galdr! It has been an absolute pleasure to be able to bring you all this knowledge so far!

**May Creation smile upon you and
bestow Her blessing on you!**

Frank A. Rúnaldrar

APPENDIXES

APPENDIX A

Table of Runic Names in Icelandic & Germanic

Rune	Numeric Value	Icelandic Name	Germanic Name
ᚠ	1	Fé	Fehu
ᚢ	2	Úr	Uruz
ᚦ	3	Þurs	Thurisaz
ᚨ	4	Óss (Ás)	Ansuz
ᚱ	5	Reið	Raidho
ᚲ	6	Kaun	Kenaz
ᚷ	7	Gjöf	Gebo
ᚹ	8	Vin	Wunjo
ᚺ	9	Hagall	Hagalaz
ᚾ	10	Nauð	Nauthiz
ᛁ	11	Íss	Isa
ᛃ	12	Ár	Jera
ᛈ	13	Perð	Pertho
ᛇ	14	Jór	Eihwaz
ᛉ	15	Ýr	Elhaz
ᛊ	16	Sól	Sowilo
ᛏ	17	Týr	Tiwaz
ᛒ	18	Bjarkan	Berkano
ᛖ	19	Eykur	Ehwaz
ᛗ	20	Maður	Mannaz
ᛚ	21	Lögur	Laguz
ᛜ	22	Ing	Ingwaz
ᛞ	23	Dagur	Dagaz
ᛟ	24	Óðal	Othala

- The Blood of Lóðurr Awakens -

APPENDIX B

References & footnotes

1. Strange Footprints on the Land (Author: Irwin, Constance publisher: Harper & Row, 1980) ISBN 0-06-022772-9)

2. Snorri Sturluson. The Prose Edda: Tales from Norse Mythology, translated by Jean I. Young (University of California Press, 1964)

3. Frank A. Rúnaldrar (2017), "The Spirit of Húnir Awakens – Part 2", London: Bastian & West. ISBN: 978-0-9955343-3-9, 'The Ultimate Trance Óðr Spirit Projection', p. 231

4. See literal translation from: http://www.voluspa.org/literal/voluspa.htm stanza 17 and 18

5. Dronke, Ursula (1997), "The Poetic Edda : Volume II : Mythological Poems", Oxford: Clarendon Press. ISBN: 978-0198111818, p. 18 and p. 124-5.

6. Thorpe, Benjamin (tr.) (1866), "Edda Sæmundar Hinns Froða : The Edda Of Sæmund The Learned", (2 vols.) London: Trübner & Co. Norroena Society edition (1905)

7. quote by – Upminster Fuller

8. Faulkes, Anthony (Trans.) (1995), "Edda. Everyman", ISBN: 0-460-87616-3, 9-10

9. Bellows, Henry Adams (1923), "The Poetic Edda", American-Scandinavian Foundation (100-101)

10. Dronke, Ursula (Trans.) (1997). "The Poetic Edda: Volume II: Mythological Poems", Oxford University Press, ISBN: 0-19-811181-9, (11)

11. Thing refers to the governing northern Germanic assembly similar in concept to our modern day Houses of Parliament. It was made up of the free people and presided by the Jarls (kings, governors and lawmakers). Still functional in Iceland and known as þing.

12. Faulkes, Anthony (Trans.) (1995), "Edda. Everyman", ISBN: 0-460-87616-3, Alivissmal, 16-17

13. See http://www.voluspa.org/alvissmal6-10.htm

14. Faulkes, Anthony (Trans.) (1998), "Edda. Everyman", ISBN: 0-460-87616-3, 12-13

15. Bellows, Henry Adams (1923), "The Poetic Edda", American-Scandinavian Foundation, 20.

16. ante p.178

17. Spa training is one of the three main forms of Seidr focussing on prophecy and foresight.

18. Part of the Hyndluljóð - Lay of Hyndla (considered to be a part of the Poetic Edda)

19. Orchard, Andy (1997), "Dictionary of Norse Myth and Legend", Cassell, ISBN: 0-304-34520-2, 78

20. Hollander, Lee M. (1962), "The Poetic Edda", Lokesenna, 100

21. See http://www.voluspa.org/alvissmal6-10.htm

22. See Dr Frisen's work (a stem cell biologist from Karolinska Institute in Stockholm). A good starter resource is the following article from the New York Times: https://www.nytimes.com/2005/08/02/science/your-body-is-younger-than-you-think.html. His

other research work can be a somewhat heavy read for those unfamiliar with neurology. Also worthy of note is Dr Lisa Ronan's research (from Cambridge Centre for Ageing and Neuroscience) on premature ageing of the brain in the overweight and obese.

23. Frank A. Rúnaldrar (2017), "The Spirit of Húnir Awakens – Part 1", London: Bastian & West, ISBN: 978-0-9955343-2-2, p.37

24. ante, 'Becoming Conscious of the Óðr', p.13

25. ante, p.37

26. Frank A. Rúnaldrar (2017), "The Spirit of Húnir Awakens – Part 2", London: Bastian & West, ISBN: 978-0-9955343-3-9, 'The Ultimate Trance Óðr Spirit Projection', p. 209

27. ante, 'The Norse 'Holy Grail'', p.223

28. ante

29. Thrope, B. (trans.) (1866), "Eddda Sæmundar Hinns Froða: Edda of Sæmund The Learned", London: Trübner & Co.

30. Marieb, EN; Hoehn, Katja (2010), "Human Anatomy & Physiology", (8th ed.), San Francisco: Benjamin Cummings, ISBN 978-0-8053-9569-3, p. 312.

31. Kienle, Alwin; Lothar Lilge; I. Alex Vitkin; Michael S. Patterson; Brian C. Wilson; Raimund Hibst; Rudolf Steiner (1 March 1996). "Why do veins appear blue? A new look at an old question". Applied Optics. 35 (7): 1151–60.Bibcode:1996ApOpt..35.1151K. doi:10.1364/AO.35.001151. PMID 21085227. Archived from the original (PDF) on 10 February 2012

32. Shmukler, Michael (2004), "Density of Blood". The Physics Factbook. Archived from the original on 19 September 2006. Retrieved 4 October 2006.

33. Alberts, Bruce (2012). "Table 22-1 Blood Cells". Molecular Biology of the Cell. NCBI Bookshelf. Archived from the original on 27 March 2018. Retrieved 1 November 2012.

34. Elert, Glenn (2012). "Volume of Blood in a Human". The Physics Factbook. His students. Archived from the original on 1 November 2012. Retrieved 2012-11-01

35. Steinsland & Meulengracht 1998:74

36. Frank A. Rúnaldrar (2017), "The Breath of Oðin Awakens", London: Bastian & West, ISBN: 978-0-9955343-4-6, p.71

37. Robinson, K., Hotopp, D. H., (2016) "Bacteria and Humans Have Been Swapping DNA for Millennia", The Scientist. Retrieved from https://www.the-scientist.com/?articles.view/articleNo/47125/title/Bacteria-and-Humans-Have-Been-Swapping-DNA-for-Millennia/irnatural

38. Yong, E. (2013), "Bacterial DNA in Human Genomes", The Scientist, retrieved from: https://www.the-scientist.com/?articles.view/articleNo/36108/title/Bacterial-DNA-in-Human-Genomes/

39. Holger Heyn, Manel Esteller, "An Adenine Code for DNA: A Second Life for N6-Methyladenine", Cell, 2015; DOI: 10.1016/j.cell.2015.04.021 https://www.sciencedaily.com/releases/2015/05/150504101254.htm

40. Millie M. Georgiadis, Isha Singh, Whitney F. Kellett, Shuichi Hoshika, Steven A. Benner, Nigel G. J. Richards, "Structural Basis for a Six Nucleotide Genetic Alphabet", Journal of the American Chemical Society, 2015; 150519090051005 DOI: 10.1021/jacs.5b03482

41. Irobalieva RN, Fogg JM, Catanese DJ, Catanese DJ, Sutthibutpong T, Chen M, Barker AK, Ludtke SJ, Harris SA, Schmid MF, Chiu W, Zechiedrich L (October 2015). "Structural diversity of supercoiled DNA". Nature Com-

munications. 6: 8440. Bibcode:2015NatCo...6E8440I. doi:10.1038/ncomms9440. PMID 26455586.

42. Venter JC, Adams MD, Myers EW, Li PW, Mural RJ, Sutton GG, et al. (February 2001). "The sequence of the human genome", Science, 291 (5507): 1304-51. doi:10.1126/science.1058040. PMID 11181995.

43. Jeane Govan, Rajendra Uprety, James Hemphill, Mark O. Lively, Alexander Deiters, "Regulation of Transcription through Light-Activation and Light-Deactivation of Triplex-Forming Oligonucleotides in Mammalian Cells", ACS Chemical Biology, 2012; 120427104811002 DOI: 10.1021/cb300161r

44. Helsingin yliopisto (University of Helsinki). (2017, April 21), "Light can be utilized to control gene function", ScienceDaily, Retrieved May 11, 2018 from www.sciencedaily.com/releases/2017/04/170421091531.htm

45. Wassermann, E.M., (2000) "Side effects of repetitive transcranial magnetic stimulation.", Depress Anxiety. 2000;12(3):124-9, PMID: 11126186, DOI: 10.1002/1520-6394(2000)12:3<124::AID-DA3>3.0.CO;2-E

46. Zwanzger P, Ella R, Keck ME, Rupprecht R, Padberg F., (2002), "Occurrence of delusions during repetitive transcranial magnetic stimulation (rTMS) in major depression.", Biol Psychiatry. 2002 Apr 1;51(7):602-3, PMID: 11950462

47. William F. N. Chan, Cécile Gurnot, Thomas J. Montine, Joshua A. Sonnen, Katherine A. Guthrie, J. Lee Nelson, "Male Microchimerism in the Human Female Brain", PLOS ONE, 2012; 7 (9): e45592 DOI: 10.1371/journal.pone.0045592

48. Frank A. Rúnaldrar (2017), "The Breath of Oðin Awakens", London: Bastian & West, ISBN: 978-0-9955343-4-6, p.42 and p.71

49. Frank A. Rúnaldrar (2017), "The Spirit of Húnir Awakens – Part 2", London: Bastian & West, ISBN: 978-0-9955343-3-9, 'The Great Mystery of Intent', p.83

50. Northwestern University, (2010, August 9), "What makes a good egg and healthy embryo? Zinc discovery may help in future fertility treatments".

51. Vries. J. de, (1956-57), "Altgermanische Religionsgeschichte. (Grundriss der germanischen Philologie 12)", Berlin: de Gruyter, Vol 1 und 2

52. Classy, R. and Vigfusson, G. (1957), "An Icelandic-English Dictionary", Oxford: Oxford University Press, p.236.

53. Grönbech, V. (1931), "The Culture of the Teutons", London: Oxford University Press

54. Originally downloaded from: http://www.heimskringla.no/wiki/Hrólfs_saga_kraka_ok_kappa_hans irnatural
English translation: Byock, Jesse L. (trans.) (1998), "The Saga of King Hrolf Kraki",. London: Penguin, ISBN 0-14-043593-X

55. Mundal, E. (1974), "fylgjemotiva i Norron Literatur", Oslo: Universitetsforlaget. Grönbech, V. (1931) "The Culture of the Teutons", London: Oxford University Press, p.1,264

56. Frank A. Rúnaldrar (2017), "The Breath of Oðin Awakens", London: Bastian & West, ISBN: 978-0-9955343-4-6.

57. See 'Dark Matter' CERN Physics. 20 January 2012 for more information.

58. Frank A. Rúnaldrar (2017), "The Spirit of Húnir Awakens – Part 1", London: Bastian & West, ISBN: 978-0-9955343-2-2, p.13

APPENDIX C

Dangers of WiFi to Human Health and DNA

Markov, M., Grigoriev, Y. G., (2013), "**Wi-Fi technology - an uncontrolled global experiment on the health of mankind**", Electromagnetic Biology and Medicine. June 2013, 32(2), 200-208, doi: 10.3109/15368378.2013.776430

Lloyds of London (Feb 2015) Very significant. Issues exclusion of liability for insurance sector from EMF (including but not limited to Wifi, Cell phone, cordless...) damage. They will not issue statements as to why.

> "The Electromagnetic Fields Exclusion (Exclusion 32) is a General Insurance Exclusion and is applied across the market as standard. The purpose of the exclusion is to exclude cover for illnesses caused by continuous long-term non-ionising radiation exposure i.e. through mobile phone usage."

see: http://emrabc.ca/wp-content/uploads/2015/03/InsuranceAE-WordingCanadav17Feb2015.pdf under: General Insurance Exclusions, 32

World Health Organisations classifies Radiofrequency Electromagnetic Fields (these include Wifi, Cell phones, Bluetooth, cordless phones and so forth) as Possibly Carcinogenic (Cancer causing) to Humans. see: International Agency for Research on Cancer – World Health Organisation, press release n.208, issued 31st May 2011 "IARC Classifies Radiofrequency Electromagnetic Fields as Possibly Carcinogenic to Humans" downloaded from: http://www.iarc.fr/en/media-centre/pr/2011/pdfs/pr208_E.pdf

Scientists & Experts Urge UN to Deal with Emerging Wireless Public Health Crisis
Scientists from 38 nations have submitted the International EMF Scientist Appeal to the United Nations, UN member states and the World Health Organization (WHO) requesting they adopt more protective exposure guidelines for electromagnetic fields (EMF) and

wireless technology in the face of increasing evidence of risk from this rapidly increasing environmental pollutant. see: leading world scientists in this field calling for a ban of Wifi and wireless technologies, see: https://www.emfscientist.org/index.php/science-policy/expert-emf-scientist-quotations for their individual comments, very insightful.

Council of Europe recommends Wi-Fi is removed from schools (see: http://assembly.coe.int/nw/xml/News/News-ViewEn.asp?newsid=3462&lang=2)

> "The Parliamentary Assembly of the Council of Europe (PACE), meeting in Kyiv at Standing Committee level, today called on European governments to "take all reasonable measures" to reduce exposure to electromagnetic fields, especially to radio frequencies from mobile phones, "and particularly the exposure to children and young people who seem to be most at risk from head tumours"."

specifically for the removal of Wi-Fi and limitation of cell (mobile) phone usage in schools:

> "According to parliamentarians, governments should "for children in general, and particularly in schools and classrooms, give preference to wired Internet connections, and strictly regulate the use of mobile phones by schoolchildren on school premises", and put in place information and awareness-raising campaigns on the risks of potentially harmful long-term biological effects on the environment and on human health, especially "targeting children, teenagers and young people of reproductive age"."

US Gov National Toxicology Program Carcinogenesis Studies findings damage to heart and brain supporting cell structures (27th May 2016)

> "hyperplastic lesions and glial cell neoplasms of heart and brain observed... likely the result of whole-body exposures to RFR" ~ Report of Partial Findings from the US Gov National Toxicology Program Carcinogenesis Studies of Cell Phone Radiofrequency Radiation in Rats (Whole Body Exposures), May 2016

The draft report of the NTP study, including comments of the peer-reviewers is available for download here: http://biorxiv.org/content/biorxiv/early/2016/05/26/055699.full.pdf

Environmental Health Trust - https://ehtrust.org
A great source of down to earth (not overly scientific) source of information on the damage of WiFi was made in an Australian program 'Wi-Fried?: Children and Wireless Devices: Does Wi-Fi harm our health?' by Dr Maryanne Demasi (see: https://ehtrust.org/wi-fried-abc-catalyst-australia-investigates-wi-fi-health-concerns/ and https://www.youtube.com/watch?v=iTNYCMlgg7E).

Dr Devra Davies from the National Institute of Enviromental Health Sciences (NIEHS): "People are assuming everything is fine until we have evidence that we are in the middle of a disaster" in a scientific presentation in Australia.

Devra Davies outline very scientific: Cell Phone Dangers | Dr. Devra Davis @ National Institute of Environmental Health Sciences (NIEHS). see: https://www.youtube.com/watch?v=wNNSztN7wJc

WiFi bans in France
Wifi is legally banned in Nursery Schools in France, severe restrictions apply in all other schools and thorough restrictions are put in place in many areas see: https://ehtrust.org/france-new-national-law-bans-wifi-nursery-school/

French National Library Bans WiFi in 2008
Scientific literature, said a library press release, "proves genotoxic effects from Wi-Fi." Human cells exposed to 2, 45 GHz, the frequency of Wi-Fi, undergo "genetic alterations," it said. (source: https://www.odwyerpr.com/story/public/6385/2016-02-23/french-national-library-banned-wi-fi-2008.html)

Belgium Bans Wifi In schools

> "Ghent's alderwoman of education and youth has banned wireless internet from spaces that cater to children between 0 and three years of age – essentially, pre-schools and day care facilities. Network cables can still be used in those facilities." (source: http://www.flanderstoday.eu/education/ghent-bans-wi-fi-pre-schools-and-day-care)

Multiple countries limiting and outright banning Wifi and Cell phones in schools (source: http://www.parentsforsafetechnology.org/worldwide-countries-taking-action.html and https://ehtrust.org/schools-worldwide-removing-wifi-reducing-exposure/)

BioInitiative 2012 - http://www.bioinitiative.org
Has a colour index of a large number of studies showing effects on practically ever key physiological function in biological systems. It is not surprising since it is an electrical system which effects another electrical system (our bodies).

Has been prepared by lead MDs and scientists in their respective fields see: http://www.bioinitiative.org/rf-color-charts/. Some notable references from the report:

DNA Damage:
- Increased cell death (apoptosis) and DNA fragmentation at 2.45 GHz for 35 days exposure (chronic exposure study), Kesari (2010)
- RFR caused genetic changes in human white blood cells, Belyaev (2005)
- 900 MHz cell phone signal induces DNA breaks and early activation of p53 gene; short exposure of 2-12 hours leads cells to acquire greater survival chance - linked to tumour aggressiveness, Marinelli (2004)
- Digital cell phone RFR at very low intensities causes DNA damage in human cells; both DNA damage and impairment of DNA is reported, Phillips (1998)

Stress increase and depression inducing damage:
- Chronic exposure to base station RF (whole-body) in humans showed increased stress hormones; dopamine levels substantially decreased; higher levels of adrenaline and,nor-adrenaline; dose-response seen; produced chronic physiological stress in cells even after 1.5 years., Buchner (2012)
- RFR affected human lymphocytes - induced stress response in cells, Sarimov (2004)
- 20 minutes of RFR at cell tower frequencies induced cell stress response, Kwee (2001)
- Increase in serum cortisol (a stress hormone), Mann 1998

Impairment or Aggression of Immune System:
- Pulsed RFR affected immune function in white blood cells, Stankiewicz (2006)
- RFR affected function of the immune system, Novoselova (1999)
- Changes in immune function, Elekes (1996)
- Immune system effects - elevation of PFC count (antibody producing cells), Veyret (1991)

Cancer:
- RFR associated with a doubling of leukemia in adults, Dolk 1997
- Changes in cell cycle; cell proliferation (960 MHz GSM mobile phone), Kwee 1997
- Lymphoma cancer rate doubled with two 1/2-hr exposures per day of cell phone radiation for 18 months (pulsed 900 MHz cell signal), Repacholi (1997)
- RFR accelerated development of both skin and breast tumors, Szmigielski (1982)

Cognitive and Sleep disruption:
- Pulse-modulated RFR and MF affect brain physiology (sleep study), Schmidt 2012
- RFR related to headache, concentration and sleeping problems, fatigue, Kundi (2009)
- Adults (18-91 yrs) with short-term exposure to GSM cell phone radiation reported headache, neurological problems, sleep and concentration problems, Hutter (2006)
- RFR caused emotional behaviour changes, free-radical damage by super-weak MWs, Akoev (2002)
- RFR from 3G cell towers decreased cognition, wellbeing, Zwamborn (2003)
- RFR from cell towers caused fatigue, headaches, sleeping problems, Navarro 2003
- Change in human brainwaves; decrease in EEG potential and statistically significant change in alpha (8-13 Hz) and beta (13-22 Hz) brainwave activity in humans at 900 MHz; exposures 6/min per day for 21 days (chronic exposure), D'Costa (2003)
- RFR caused changes in hippocampus (brain memory and learning), Tattersall (2001)

- Cell phone use results in changes in cognitive thinking/mental tasks related to memory retrieval, Krause (2000)
- An 18% reduction in REM sleep (important to memory and learning functions), Mann (1996)
- RFR caused impaired nervous system activity, Dumansky (1974)

Effects in Children:
- In children and adolescents (8-17 yrs) short-term exposure caused headache, irritation, concentration difficulties in school, Heinrich (2010)
- In children and adolescents (8-17 yrs) short-term exposure caused conduct problems in school (behavioural problems), Thomas (2010)
- RFR decreased survival in children with leukemia, Hocking 2000
- RFR caused a two-fold increase in leukemia in children, Hocking 1996
- Memory impairment, slowed motor skills and retarded learning in children, Chiang (1989)

FORTHCOMING TITLES

The Self Awakens
The Roadmap to High Galdr

Mastering runes is an ongoing task many undertake but few achieve. In this book you will find all the elementary skills needed to master High Galdr and unleash the full power of the runes. Rune mastery starts with the development and unification of the Self; without knowledge of the Self, mastery of rune use is impossible. It is only with the understanding and mastery of our Self that actual rune mastery can begin.

In here you will find essential basics of the teachings from *The Breath of Oðin Awakens*, *The Spirit of Húnir Awakens (Parts 1 & 2)* and *The Blood of Lóðurr Awakens*, providing a quick guide to help you develop the skills and abilities you need for High Galdr. Learn about the Breath (Önd), the Megin (archetypal force or power) and Hamingja, the Spirit (Óðr), Mind (Hugr), Memory (Minni), Shadow Self (Sal), Energy Body or 'soul' (Hamr), physical body (Lik) and how to wield them runically.

Mastering these fundamental parts of your Self will enable you to start using the runes, their characteristics, power, energies and influences across multiple levels of reality.

An essential guide for those who have not progressed through the *The Breath of Odin Awakens*, *The Spirit of Húnir Awakens (Parts 1 & 2)* and *The Blood of Lóðurr Awakens* and want to cover the minimal foundational practice for High Galdr.

High Galdr: Rune Science
The Sacred Science of the Gods

Runes, runes and more runes! The sacred science of the Gods, the runes were made available to their children, our Ancestors. Much information is available about the runes, yet so very little is known as to how they are actually used. They are chanted, they are written, and they are drawn. Yet all these methods fail to produce rapid or tangible manifestations.

Using the runes is a science and, like any science, the rules under which its principles operate need to be known. Unleashing a runic vocalisation using proper Galdr has been kept secret for ages, known to only an extremely select few who were capable of mastering their very Self. These methods for Galdr were passed down through generations as part of our vocal tradition, with only sparse written instruction preserved.

At long last, actual methods and underlying principles of manifesting the power of the runes are being made available unabridged with no hidden facets, no secret methods left unturned. Learn at long last how to wield the runes, how to unleash and manifest them, how to recode reality and reform events in life using the heritage left to us by our Ancestors and living with-in our DNA. Each and every rune holds a secret, a key, a power, a source of knowledge and a potential.

Learn to unleash it ALL with actual High Galdr.

- The Blood of Lóðurr Awakens -

www.ingramcontent.com/pod-product-compliance
Lightning Source LLC
Chambersburg PA
CBHW032037150426
43194CB00006B/319